Bilingual Books – Biliterate Children
learning to read through dual language books

Raymonde Sneddon

Trentham Books
in partnership with Mantra Lingua
Stoke on Trent and London, UK

Trentham Books Limited

Westview House   22883 Quicksilver Drive
734 London Road   Sterling
Oakhill   VA 20166-2012
Stoke on Trent   USA
Staffordshire
England ST4 5NP

First published 2009

British Library Cataloguing-in-Publication Data
A catalogue record for this book is available from the British Library

ISBN: 978 1 85856 460 9

Cover illustrations taken from: *We're Going on a Bear Hunt* by Michael Rosen and Helen Oxenbury, reproduced by permission of Walker Books Ltd, London – Cover illustration copyright © 1989 Helen Oxenbury; *Handa's Hen* by Eileen Browne, reproduced by permission of Walker Books Ltd, London – Cover illustration copyright © 2002 Eileen Browne; and *The Giant Turnip* by Henriette Barkow and Richard Johnson reproduced by permission of Mantra Lingua, London – Cover illustration copyright © 2001 Richard Johnson

Designed and typeset by Trentham Books Ltd and printed in Great Britain by Page Bros (Norwich) Ltd, Norfolk.

Contents

Acknowledgements • vi

Introduction • vii

Chapter 1
Context and history • 1

Chapter 2
Language use and literacy practices in families and communities • 27

Chapter 3
Issues in identity • 43

Chapter 4
Issues in translation • 55

Chapter 5
Magda and Albana • 69

Chapter 6
The *suraj*, the sun, is inside the *mashriq*, and it comes out • 85

Chapter 7
Practice, pleasure and persistence • 99
Collaborative learning in Turkish

Chapter 8
Sarah the reader • 113

Chapter 9
Mohammed – learning to read in Gujarati • 127

Chapter 10
Bilingual books – biliterate children? • 141

Appendix
Practical ideas for the classroom: further reading • 149

Website resources • 151

References • 155

Index • 163

For Hilary Hester Ives, who changed my life as a teacher

Acknowledgements

This book builds on a long engagement with dual language books: reading them, researching them and making them with children (including my own) and their families. In the course of that journey I have been inspired and encouraged by many teachers encountered on the way who shared my interest. Jacqui Clover and Sue Gilbert started me off on the book-making journey. Luisa Pieris joined me on the Mother and Child Writing Group and we shared the pleasures of collaborative book-making with children and their mothers at Jubilee School.

More recent inspiration came from the many colleagues who participated in the Dual Language Action Research Project at the University of East London from 2002 to 2004 and explored so many innovative ideas for developing multilingual learning in the classroom.

I am greatly indebted to the colleagues who introduced me to the children and parents who made this research project possible: Samina Jaffar, Navneet Padda, Mita Kurana and Catherine Coop, encountered through the Developing Reading Skills Through Home Languages Project in the London Borough of Redbridge and Kathryn Kabra, through the UEL Action Research Group. I would like to thank them and all the staff who facilitated my field work in schools.

Teachers, researchers, artists, story tellers and publishers involved in the development of dual language books have contributed to this work. I would like to thank Eve Gregory, Roger Hancock, Keya Ashraf, James Ma, Janet Campbell, Amanda and John Welch, Jean Conteh, Mishti Chatterji, Robene Dutta, Jennie Mechti, Usha Bahl, Claire John and Camilla Baker for the time they took to share their memories and experiences and for bringing the story of dual language books to life.

While I have developed some strong language awareness strategies over the many years I have worked in multilingual schools, I do not speak all the languages used in this research project. I am very grateful for the expert advice on language issues from Valbona Selmani, Kanta Patel, Fizza Butt, Zohra Sardar and Atakan Mercan.

I would like to thank Keya Ashraf of Chadpur Press and Mishti Chatterji from Mantra Lingua for permission to use illustrations on the cover of the book and in the text.

My late colleague Peter Martin was passionate about languages and we had made many plans for research to develop further the issues explored in this study. I greatly miss his advice and support. My editor Gillian Klein believed in this project from the moment I contacted her and I thank her for guiding me safely through the final stages of producing the manuscript.

My family have supported me with love, patience and faith that the work would eventually get completed: to Peter, Denis and Gavin with love and thanks for being there for me throughout.

But the greatest investment of commitment and time came from the children who are the subject of the present research and their mothers: Magda, Albana, Lere and Miranda, Mydda and Bismah, Lek, Durkan and Sarah, Mohammed and Farhana, acknowledged here under the pseudonyms they chose for themselves. Their dedication to and enthusiasm for bilingual learning and the creativity they brought to the task of learning to read using dual language books made the research project an enriching and very enjoyable experience.

Introduction

'You add -*an* and it makes it bigger', explains Lek. 'If you spell zürafada, that's just a giraffe, but if you add -*an*, it makes it like, more popular, it's like there's more giraffes.'

His friend Durkan intervenes to suggest that this addition means bigger and Lek expands: 'if you have, like, connectives and stuff, it makes the word bigger'.

Lek and Durkan are reading the dual language version of *The Giant Turnip* (Barkow, 2002) in Turkish and English. They are working to-gether to understand the texts and are keen to share their expertise and explain to me how 'connectives and stuff' work in Turkish.

Lek and Durkan are two of the children who took part in a project to explore how young bilingual children interact with text when they are reading simultaneously in their two languages. The other children in the study are Magda and Albana, who speak Albanian, Mydda who speaks Urdu and some Punjabi, Mohammed who speaks Gujarati and Sarah who speaks French and understands Lingala.

When I was introduced to the children by their teachers, Magda, Albana, Mohammed and Mydda were learning to read with their mothers in the language spoken at home, Lek and Durkan were teaching each other and Sarah was teaching herself. They were all using the picture books published in two languages which were in their schools.

The children live in east London boroughs. In the three primary schools they attend, most of the children are bilingual and, between them, speak many different languages at home. The children's teachers value their language skills and have encouraged them to become biliterate.

This book is for such teachers. Teachers who enjoy exploring languages and learning from classroom based research and observation, whether they teach English as an additional language, develop the languages children use at home or teach them new ones. It has grown from my commitment to learning and sharing languages in the classroom, through working closely with families to use and make dual language books and other multilingual materials over a period of over thirty years. It has been inspired by the many colleagues I have worked with in the course of being a teacher, a teacher educator and a researcher through formal and informal action research projects and activities.

In the 1980s I learned the value of action research when I participated in the Language in the Multicultural Primary Classroom project, directed by Hilary Hester. The more immediate inspiration for my recent work came from an action research project based in the Cass School of Education at the University of East London (UEL). A group of primary school teachers met regularly from 2002 to 2004 to experiment with multilingual resources in the classroom and share innovative practice (Sneddon, 2007). Support for several of the case studies reported here came from a project developed by the Minority Ethnic Achievement Service of the London Borough of Redbridge entitled *Developing Reading Skills through Home Languages Project* (EMAT, 2008). In this project the schools' own reading programmes were complemented with dual language books to help pupils develop reading skills in their home languages with the support of their parents.

This introductory chapter provides information about the educational context in which the children are learning to become biliterate and about new opportunities for developing language learning. It includes an outline of the aims and methodology of the project, the research issues in language and identity that are directly relevant to the children's experiences and an outline of the structure and content of the volume.

The languages spoken by the children in the present study are generally referred to as 'community languages'. But I have called them 'home languages' or 'languages of the home' throughout the book as they are the ones spoken in the children's homes on a daily basis, even though others, including English, may be used at home for various purposes.

The educational context

The seven children who feature in this study are in many ways typical of bilingual children in UK schools. The population of children who use a language other than English in the home has been growing steadily throughout the United Kingdom since the 1960s. At the time of writing it is close to 700,000 pupils. While most of this population is concentrated in large cities, recent immigrants from Eastern Europe have also moved into rural areas and few schools can now claim that they have never encountered a bilingual child. London itself is the most multilingual city in the world: children in London schools speak more than 300 languages (Baker and Eversley, 2000).

Children who use more than one language in their everyday lives belong to communities who have arrived in the UK at different stages. In the 1960s and 1970s most migration originated from the New Commonwealth countries and the second and third generations of the children, like Mohammed and Mydda, are now in the schools. Throughout the 1990s many of the new-comers came as refugees from zones of conflict, like the families of Sarah, Magda and Albana. More recently still, the growth of the European Union has encouraged new arrivals to come to the UK in search of employment oppor-tunities and an increasing number have brought their children and settled. The role of London as an international centre for business and finance ensures that there is always a large settlement of families from the countries of the original European Union.

In the face of this multilingual population the education policies of the UK have historically been assimilationist (Townsend, 1971; Conteh *et al*, 2007), with the focus being on teaching English to 'immigrant' children, with little notice taken of the languages they spoke.

In the early 1980s the Inner London Education Authority (ILEA) recognised the value of the bilingualism of its pupils. Courses at the Centre for Urban Educational Studies prepared teachers for working in multicultural schools and encouraged action research in the classroom and the development of multilingual resources. Peripatetic teachers of community languages were deployed to teach in mainstream schools. Similar educational developments occurred in industrial cities such as Bradford. The Linguistic Minorities Pro-ject (LMP, 1985) made policy makers and teachers aware of the prevalence and use of minority languages and the ways in which communities organised to teach their children. However in the same year the Swann report into the education of children from new communities, *Education for All* (DES, 1985), recommended that the teaching of community languages should be the res-ponsibility of the communities themselves. The ILEA was abolished in 1989 and with it most of its specialist teachers' centres and the Mother Tongue teaching team.

The National Curriculum of 1989 was resolutely anglocentric and mono-lingual. It left very little space in its overcrowded syllabus and re-introduced a strongly assimilationist approach to teaching bilingual pupils. While a later version (DfEE, 2000) refers to building on children's experiences of community languages, it provides little encouragement or advice as to how teachers may do this.

More recently the *Aiming High* documents on the education of pupils from ethnic minority communities have been positive about bilingualism (DfES, 2003). Reports from Ofsted (the body responsible for the inspection of schools) acknowledge the research on the benefits of bilingualism and recommend that schools make use of the skills that pupils have in community languages (Ofsted, 2005). The Primary Strategy's *Learning and Teaching for Bilingual Children in the Primary Years* (DfES, 2006) refers to research on the transfer of skills from one language to another and it also advises building on children's language knowledge. It specifically recommends the use of dual language books in the classroom and a close engagement with pupils' families and the wider community.

The positive messages about bilingualism in recent policy documents are slow to make an impact in the day-to-day life of schools. It is rare to hear a language other than English spoken by pupils in class, or even in the playground. Pupils seem to have read the invisible notice on the classroom wall that says 'English only' (Cummins, 2007). Language shift and loss can be rapid as the children internalise the negative values accorded to their languages and this can cause families great concern. Few children in the UK outside of Wales (which has a bilingual education policy) have the opportunity to learn bilingually in their mainstream schools. For most children, becoming literate in the language of the home either involves learning at home or attending complementary school. Even when parents are keen, willing and able to teach their children to read, as were the parents of the children in the present study, the demands of work and family and the lack of teaching resources and children's books can make this a difficult task.

Complementary schools run classes in the evenings or at weekends. They are organised by communities themselves in response to need; almost all are seriously underfunded and many are staffed by volunteers. Children can benefit greatly from learning in an environment that values and develops their language skills, supports their achievement in the mainstream and provides a space that enables them to explore their personal identity (Kenner *et al*, 2008a). However the small number of teaching hours (commonly two to four per week) and the generally poor resourcing of the complementary sector, highlight the difference in status between the languages and English. Until very recently, complementary schools (also known as Saturday schools, mother-tongue schools, community schools) were largely unknown outside the communities which they serve and relationships with mainstream schools were rare.

New opportunities for language learning?

While the focus of the present study is on children who are learning to be literate in the community language that their families speak at home, what can be learned from observing the children could have a wider application in view of changes in the language teaching curriculum.

Until recently, languages other than English taught in schools have fallen into two categories: the Modern Foreign Languages (MFL) taught as part of the National Curriculum (most commonly French, Spanish and German) and Community Languages. This term is generally used in the UK to describe languages spoken by immigrant communities. The terminology has become increasingly irrelevant as distinctions have blurred. For example more community languages are available as MFLs at examination level (Ofsted, 2008); some, like Chinese and Arabic are strongly promoted for commercial purposes; French is spoken by communities, like Sarah's, who have come from francophone Africa.

The *National Languages Strategy* (DfES, 2002) provides an entitlement for all pupils to learn another language and specifies that any language may be taught. The recently published document, *Positively Plurilingual* (CILT, 2007), celebrates the language diversity of the school population. It promotes the concept of English Plus and encourages schools to develop pupils' knowledge of languages and teach a much wider range. A recent project funded by the Department for Children, Schools and Families (DCSF), aims to promote the teaching of community languages and to encourage complementary and mainstream schools to work together (CILT, 2008). The project is entitled 'Our Languages', in a deliberate attempt to break down the distinction between community and MFL languages. More recently, the Training and Development Agency for Schools (TDA) has adopted the term 'world languages'. However, French and Spanish are still the languages most commonly taught in schools and many schools are unaware that they have the option of teaching the languages children speak at home.

It would be naïve to consider that a few sentences in a policy document can undo decades of devaluing community languages and challenge the power of prestigious European languages in the curriculum. Pupils are very aware of this: a Kurdish and Arabic speaker, recently arrived from Iraq, commented on the usefulness of her languages: 'Miss, who needs the languages of immigrants? You need to be good at English, very good at English.' (Mehmedbegovic, 2007). Two of the schools attended by the children in the study are introducing French and Mohammed, in particular, is proud of what he has learned. Although they value the children's home languages, none of these schools has introduced teaching in any of the languages spoken by the many bilingual children who attend them. However when the school attended by Magda and Albana introduced a lunch-time Albanian club because of their enthusiasm and success, non-Albanian speaking children also joined, keen to learn some of their friends' language and energetic traditional dances.

While there are essential differences in pedagogy involved in teaching new languages, there are also opportunities to consider areas of commonality. Brown (2007) has drawn attention to the links between pedagogy for teaching English as an additional language (EAL), the Key Stage 2 *Framework for Languages and the Primary Framework for Literacy.* Conteh has highlighted the generic skills involved in language learning (2008). She has expressed concern at the lack of an understanding of principles common to language development and learning due to the fact that different aspects, such as EAL, MFL, Community Languages and Literacy in English, are separate curriculum specialisms, often taught by different people to children in primary schools and by different lecturers to student teachers (Conteh, forthcoming). Initiatives like CILT's Our Languages project and the research into community languages and complementary schools (Creese *et al*, 2008), funded by the Economic and Social Research Council (ESRC), provide a positive context in which new pedagogies can be explored. Two recent projects have explored bilingual teaching strategies in primary schools in Tower Hamlets, using Bengali and English (Kenner *et al*, 2008b). The National Association for Language Development in the Curriculum (NALDIC: the professional organisation of teachers of EAL) are exploring principles and practice in bilingual pedagogy (Cable *et al*, 2009).

Both the teachers who took part in the UEL based Action Research project and those who worked on the Redbridge Project were trying out strategies and developing resources to support bilingual pupils in their learning of literacy in English and in the languages of their home. They developed materials that could be used in different contexts to encourage children to explore and share languages and interest them in language learning. Some of these issues are explored in this book with specific reference to dual language books as one widely available multilingual resource.

Aims, methodology and research context

A review of relevant research and personal experience of the UEL Action Research and Redbridge Projects and of classroom practice suggested the following research questions for a small exploratory ethnographic study:

- what can close observation of children learning to read using dual language books reveal about the transfer of concepts and skills?
- does the relationship between English and the home language affect the ease and nature of the transfer?
- does reading two texts simultaneously have an impact on children's understanding of how language works and on their comprehension of a text?
- does learning to read dual language books have an impact on the development of learner and personal identity?

The children were identified by colleagues who had encouraged parents to read dual language books with their children. They arranged the initial contact with parents to discuss the project and to arrange suitable times and venues for meeting. Semi-structured interviews with parents were used to obtain information about family language use and literacy practices. Information was also obtained from teachers about the children's literacy development in class. The Albanian, Urdu and Gujarati speaking children were observed reading with their mothers at a time and place convenient to them. The French and Turkish children were observed reading in school. All interviews and observations were transcribed. The transcriptions, field notes and draft chapters were discussed with mothers and children and advice was obtained on language issues arising from parents and expert colleagues. Between four and six observations were carried out for each child within a flexible time scale to accommodate school and family priorities.

Cummins argues that building on pupils' cultural knowledge and language skills and providing teaching that 'affirms their identities and enables them to invest their identities in learning' (Cummins *et al*, 2006:3) enables successful academic engagement. His empowerment model (Cummins, 1986, 2000), familiar to all the teachers involved in the present study, provided an overall framework for exploring the impact of supporting children's home languages in school. The study is focused around the transfer of skills between the languages the children use and was informed by Cummins' concept of the Common Underlying Proficiency (1984, 1991) and Bialystok's work on the transfer of skills between different pairs of languages (1997, 2001, 2004).

Of particular relevance to the present study is the current research on the development of multiliteracy (Kenner, 2000), and the concept of syncretic literacy (Gregory *et al*, 2004; Gregory, 2008b). The role of parents in the development of their children's multiliteracy is crucial and the work was informed by studies of home literacy practices (Gregory and Williams, 2000; Martin-Jones and Jones, 2000; Kenner, 2000a, 2006b) and of families' 'funds of knowledge' (Gonzalez *et al*, 1993).

The exploration of children's identities built on work on multidimensional personal and learner identities by Pavlenko and Blackledge (2004) and by Creese *et al* (2006) in the context of complementary schools.

The study was informed by research on dual language texts in the English context: the major exploration of their use by the Multilingual Resources for Children Project (MRC, 1995) and Viv Edwards' work at the University of Reading, the observational study of Ming-Tsow (1986) and more recent case studies by Sneddon and Patel (2003), Robertson (2006) and Ma (2008) as well as Edwards and Walker's paper on the translation of dual language books (1996). Also relevant to the study is the recent work on the translation of children's literature (Lathey, 2006). A full discussion of the research that informed the project is to be found in Chapters 1 to 4.

The structure of the book

The book reports on an exploratory study of bilingual children learning to read in the language of the home from a text in two languages. It was carried out by a researcher only fluent in one of the five languages spoken by the children, with the assistance of bilingual parents and colleagues. The study reveals the individual variation and complexity of a child's multilingual and multiliterate experience. It shows how much of this can be discovered by a teacher or researcher who does not share the language of the child, and should demonstrate to teachers in this situation that they can still support the children's language learning and find out a great deal about language themselves in the process. However it is hoped that the study will encourage more teachers (like Navneet Padda who taught Magda and Albana) and researchers (like James Ma) who do share the languages of the children to explore the issues from a different perspective and in the much greater depth that their language skills would allow.

The book has been structured in two sections.

Section I – Dual Language books: practice and research

Chapter 1 follows the dual language books from the early 1980s, as they developed to meet the needs of the children who used them, and how they were endlessly reinvented, in small school-based projects, larger specially funded-projects, commercial publication and, finally, on the internet. In addition to the use of published books, the making of dual language books by children, the identity texts that reflect their personal experience, anticipated the Family Learning movement and have provided one of the most powerful ways for teachers to learn about the challenges, advantages and limitations of dual language books. The chapter includes interview data from teachers and publishers who developed books in distinctive ways.

Chapter 2 considers the different forms of bilingualism most likely to be encountered in the UK and their effect on language use and literacy practice relevant to the simultaneous reading of text in two languages. It explores research into the transfer of reading skills in bilingual children, studies that consider how children make sense of the different forms of literacy they encounter in different environments in school, home and community, and the role played by family members in the process.

Chapter 3 considers issues of personal identity and the importance for children of finding their own cultures and language reflected in the materials available in school. It looks at how different types of books produced for different audiences and purposes can meet or fail this requirement and the implications for their wider use in the classroom. The chapter also explores the value to children of making their own books based on personal experience and their own voice.

Chapter 4 considers issues in translation. It is rare for those who have never been involved in translating texts to be aware of the many layers of complexity and difficulty involved. The translation of children's literature raises many interesting questions about audience, purpose and culture (Lathey, 2006). The chapter looks into some of the additional choices and challenges involved in translating texts for publication as dual language books.

Section II – the stories

The second part of this book presents five case studies of children learning to read: Magda and Albana in Albanian, Lek and Durkan in Turkish, Mydda in Urdu, Mohammed in Gujarati and Sarah in French. Issues explored include the strategies children use when reading two texts simultaneously, the nature of the transfer of skills between the two languages, the impact on children's metalinguistic understanding and comprehension of a story and the implications for children's evolving personal and learner identities.

I was invited into three schools by colleagues who had either participated in the UEL Action Research project or who were part of the Redbridge Literacy Project. They introduced me to children who were learning to read in the language of the home using the dual language books, either with their parents at home or by helping each other. I was invited to meet their families to explain the project and to work out with them the best procedure for studying their children's biliteracy development.

As one of the aims was to study the transfer of reading skills from one language to another, children were chosen whose languages presented a different relationship with English, through different writing systems and different scripts. The six languages represent three different scripts and three writing systems: English, Albanian, Turkish and French use the Roman script and an alphabetic system, Urdu uses the Perso-Arabic script and a consonantal system and Gujerati uses the Devanagari script and a syllabic system. The languages also vary in their syntactic structure, morphology, syllable structure and the consistency of their spelling system.

As well as different home languages, the children had different levels of competence in reading English, varying expertise in and opportunities to use their home language. What all of them had in common was the lack of opportunity to develop their personal bilingualism through attendance at classes whether in school time or outside of school, and little access to children's books in the family language other than the dual language books supplied by the school.

Each of the five chapters in this second section tells the story of the very different ways in which children and parents approached the task of learning to read in the language of the community.

Chapter 5: in school A, six year-old Magda and Albana had been learning to read in Albanian with their mothers for six months before I met them. The study follows the girls as they negotiate meaning across languages with their mothers, develop their understanding of Albanian text, join the top group in their class for reading in English, and develop great pride in their biliteracy.

Three children were originally observed learning Urdu with their mothers in School B. Chapter 6 tells the story of how seven year-old Mydda, from being a competent but reluctant reader in English, became passionate about cracking the code that would enable her to read in Urdu. In the process she rediscovered her love of the rhymes and stories that her mother used to tell her.

Chapter 7: Lek and Durkan were eight years old when I was invited to meet them in School C to observe them helping each other to read in Turkish. Their collaborative approach and the discussions they had revealed the strategies they used to make sense of print and to understand how their different languages worked.

Chapter 8: in school C I also met Sarah, aged nine, who spoke French and English and understood Lingala, a language from the Democratic Republic of Congo. Sarah was a talented and enthusiastic reader. She was proud of having taught herself to read in French from dual language books and enjoyed exploring stories beyond the immediate meaning on the page.

Chapter 9: later in the project I met Mohammed who was in the same class as Magda and Albana. A voracious reader in English, he was learning to read with his mother in Gujarati. He enjoyed exploring the stories orally in two languages, and was only just beginning to master the Gujarati script.

All of the children in the project launched into learning to read in the language of the home as a result of being offered the books by teachers in their schools. Both they and the parents involved were enthusiastic about the resources. However the study shows that few other books for children were available to them. The study considers which aspects of the books helped the children in their learning as well as the limitations of their use and the additional and alternative materials that were needed to support their developing biliteracy.

Clearly identified in the study is the crucial role that schools and teachers, both monolingual and bilingual, played in removing the invisible 'English Only' sign from their classroom walls through valuing children's language learning and providing the necessary support and resources. Chapter 10 draws together some conclusions from the research project and offers some suggestions and resources that may provide starting points for teachers and researchers new to the complex and exciting research and pedagogical opportunities offered by the developing multilingual classroom.

1
Context and history

A lasting memory is of one three year-old in the nursery. She became so attached to the book written for her that she could not bear to put it down, even in the busy classroom. Her solution? She carried it around in her mouth, with the teeth-marks proudly decorating the cover to prove its value and importance. (Clover and Gilbert, 1981:9)

Teachers know that children treasure books made for them from their own experience. The story of dual language books in British schools over the last thirty years provides an interesting account of teachers' creativity and pragmatism. As they were faced with more and more children from all over the world who spoke many languages but little English, teachers found ways of meeting children's needs and engaging them actively in language learning. The accounts of different projects described below demonstrate the clear sense of purpose behind them, the strong sense of audience, the networks of colleagues, family and friends on which they drew and the strong links with children's families and communities that developed as a result. Teachers spent hours planning, contacting families, building relationships, cutting and pasting on their kitchen tables before word-processing was readily available. In the course of this work they discovered that, while the books were a valued resource for children, the process of making them was enriching for all who were involved in it.

A full history of dual language books is beyond the scope of the present volume. This first chapter provides a few snapshots of developments in bilingual book-making from 1980 to the present. The stories told, based on personal experience and interviews with colleagues, demonstrate how, while each book-making project had a specific purpose and audience and was grounded in a particular time and place, ideas have been shared, lost and rediscovered, adapted and developed by others, to meet the needs of different children in different times and places.

Books published in community languages and English have been in use in some multilingual schools in England since the 1970s. As more children arrived from an ever greater range of countries of origin and classrooms became increasingly multilingual, pedagogies were developed to support the learning of English. In-service courses, such as those provided by the Centre for Urban Educational Studies in London, were designed to provide teachers with an understanding of the cultures, language and learning needs and communities of the new arrivals and with strategies for teaching English effectively in mixed mainstream classrooms. As teachers became aware of the importance of supporting and valuing pupils' first languages, many started making their own dual language books, working with bilingual colleagues and involving parents through writing workshops of various kinds.

The following stories provide some examples of the processes by which dual language resources were produced, the purposes for which they were made, their advantages and drawbacks and the wider implications of their use in the classroom. The original purpose of the books was generally to help children learn English and gain access to texts used for teaching reading in the classroom, but they also aimed to value their family language and cultural experiences by making these visible in the classroom.

In some cases dual language books made in school were aimed at a particular language group, in others they were designed to be accessible to children speaking many languages. The same principles applied to books developed in a more professional manner through funding obtained for special projects, some of them tied to a research agenda. The high quality and success of some of the books produced as well as the advent of user friendly multilingual word processing software encouraged commercial ventures publishing books for a wider market. New multimedia technology has led to new multilingual developments and the sharing of resources once dependent on the photocopier has been revolutionised by the internet.

Teachers, parents and children making books in school
Book making in a Tower Hamlets School
Jacqui Clover and Sue Gilbert, who taught in a school in which ten languages were spoken, described the purpose of their book making as 'using the rich language and cultural backgrounds of our families as a resource for the school' (1981:6). The teachers developed strong partnerships with parents as

they supported them to write individual books with and about their own children, reflecting the children's personal experience. The books were pro-duced, not as dual language books, but in parallel versions in both English and the language of the child's home. Stories about everyday life, significant events, or the home country, were printed in multiple copies for the child to keep and for other children to find in the class and school library. Children and parents illustrated, teachers and parents cut, pasted, photocopied and laminated. Books were made in Bengali, Urdu, Gujarati, French, Greek and English.

Clover and Gilbert, in evaluating their work, note the beneficial outcomes: 'the books have helped to extend good home/school links and to establish a true multicultural curriculum' (*op cit*:9). They also demonstrate the great value children placed on their personal books as evidenced by the behaviour of the nursery child described in the opening paragraph of this chapter.

Through running workshops for teachers and publishing an account of their work, the two teachers inspired many others to follow their example and adapt their model to benefit the children in their own school.

Book making in a Hackney School

The Mother and Child Writing Project (Sneddon, 1986a) was one example. In a school in which over twenty languages were spoken, weekly workshops were run for bilingual mothers to make dual language books with their own children. The project was piloting new software that enabled the community language to be word processed alongside English (Sneddon, 1986b). In the first two years of its development, it benefited from the presence in work-shops of Kulwant Chadda, a bilingual teacher of English to Speakers of Other Languages, provided by the local Further Education College. Children learned to write in English and their home language; mothers who spoke little English were able to participate, develop their language skills and learn word processing with their children. Books were produced in print runs of twenty for distribution to parents and within the school. A formal book launch with invited guests was organised by participating mothers at the end of each phase of the project. The purpose of the project had been to value and en-courage bilingualism and biliteracy. The teachers who ran the workshops noted the substantial benefits to the children's literacy development, to their confidence and pride and the great value they placed on these personal books.

The development of writing workshops

While dual language books have developed and a wide range is now available commercially in many languages, the making of personal books in school, either with children and parents, or targeted at the needs of a particular group of pupils, is a popular activity. While it is time-consuming for teachers, the process of book-making, as Clover and Gilbert found, brings many benefits to children in terms of language development, motivation, confidence in their own developing bilingualism and biliteracy and pride in their achievements. The partnership with parents brings to the school the benefit of their expertise and knowledge and strengthens the home-school relationship.

As another benefit of bookmaking activities involving parents was often an improvement in parents' own use of English, a number of schools sought funding to run literacy workshops for families. The Basic Skills Unit recognised the benefit of these and funded a number of projects (Brooks *et al*, 1996). More recently, the research of James Ma (2008) into a mother and child reading a dual language book in Chinese and English emerged directly from his involvement in a family learning programme. Individual teachers have continued to rediscover this formula for themselves and developed it in innovative directions to meet the specific needs in their school: an example from the London Borough of Waltham Forest demonstrates what student teachers can learn from working in a mother and child literacy workshop (Kabra, 2007). Working in a West Country community with substantial numbers of Nepali families for whom no bilingual resources were available, Camilla Baker used the workshop model to develop a resource of Nepali-English books which were made available online. A school in Bristol with substantial numbers of Somali speaking children developed *Abdi and the Hyena*, a traditional Somali tale, as a home-school project and published an attractively designed dual language book illustrated by the children (John, 2007).

School-based translations

In the absence of commercially produced dual language books, or indeed in the absence of funding to buy them once they were available, handwritten translations of well loved picture books, such as *Mr Gumpy's Outing* (Burningham, 1984), were widely produced in primary classrooms. This involved a process by which bilingual teachers, classroom assistants, parents and friends were roped in to provide translations which were then copied and made available to children alongside the English text.

The main purpose of this approach was to enable pupils to gain access to key texts used in the classroom for story telling and teaching reading and to support their learning of English. The aim was that children literate in their own language would be able to read the translations. Those who could not would take the books home to be read by their parents. The amateur translators were sometimes encouraged to make tapes of their texts so that children could listen to them in school.

One major disadvantage of this procedure was the endless reinvention of the wheel by many teachers. There must have been dozens of versions of *The Very Hungry Caterpillar* (Carle, 1992) in circulation at any given time in the main languages spoken by newly arrived children, all of them produced by amateur translators.

Where language support teachers employed by the Local Education Authority were deployed in schools with substantial numbers of bilingual children in the London area, they encouraged teachers to save time by sharing resources. Translations into key languages (in the 1980s these were generally Urdu, Punjabi, Gujarati, Hindi, Bengali, Greek and Turkish) started circulating, printed, page by page, on sticky labels which teachers stuck into extra copies of the texts bought for the purpose. The books were criticised for the often flawed translations and the negative message they conveyed about the value of community languages, as soon-to-peel-off labels in handwritten scripts were stuck alongside properly printed English text. There were real pitfalls to this approach: many a teacher ended up with the sticky label on the wrong page, and even (and this happened particularly with Hindi and Punjabi) with the text inserted upside down.

However, in spite of criticism and the occasional egg on a teacher's face, children and parents were positive about these books. Parents used them with their children and were willing to come in to school to read them. They recorded audio tapes to go alongside them in classroom listening corners and they were willing for these to be copied in Teachers' Centres and shared with schools across London.

At school level, the effort that individual teachers put in to produce multilingual resources conveyed to children and their parents the value that the teachers placed on their language. Translating, making tapes, coming in to school to read a story in Urdu or Bengali, making captions for school books and displays, advising on resources and cultural events in school, all of these activities put a value on the parents' funds of personal and cultural knowledge. They engaged parents in the school as partners, involving them more closely in their children's education. While there were obvious benefits for the school in helping them to engage with the real life linguistic and cultural experience of the children and their families, there were great benefits to children who found their parents more knowledgeable and confident to support their education at home. The developing partnerships in some cases led parents to training courses in education, employment as teaching assistants, and to becoming school governors.

Examples of this type of partnership occurred in the present study: the mothers of Mohammed, Albana and Magda all volunteered to help regularly in their children's classroom. Two of them proceeded to study for qualifications, Mohammed's mother as a teaching assistant and Albana's as a nursery assistant.

While the original purpose of translating books may have been to help children gain access to English texts and value their home language, the process of doing this had the considerable added value of building partnerships between the school and parents who may not otherwise have engaged with it.

With the main purpose of helping children to understand what a book used in class was about, Janet Campbell rediscovered (and upgraded) the sticky label approach in a project carried out in Haringey in the 1990s. She was inspired to launch the project in nursery classes when she observed a mother reading a picture book to her child at the end of the day 'I noticed that one Iranian mother was simultaneously translating into Farsi as she read the book. The child now knows what the book is about' (Campbell, 2008).

In the context of a concern about the underachievement of children of Turkish heritage, the project aimed to support children's understanding by having all of the 25 core books used in nursery classrooms translated into Turkish. The text was typed in Turkish font onto adhesive labels and stuck into additional copies of the books bought for the purpose. In several schools an after-school library was set up, staffed by a Turkish speaking teaching assistant who invited parents to take the books home and read them to their children (Colledge and Campbell, 1997).

The project was popular with parents and continued in some schools for several years. While Campbell's main aim was to support children's understanding of texts used in the English classroom, she was delighted at the opportunities the project provided to engage parents in discussion about their children's language and literacy development and the importance of maintaining the use of the Turkish language in the home.

Issues of translation loom large in the evaluation of dual language books and of their impact on those who use them; a chapter of this book is devoted to discussing them. They were significant in Campbell's project which was aiming to address the needs of children speaking Turkish from a range of backgrounds: mainland Turkey, Cypriot Turkish and London Turkish. Differences in grammar and vocabulary produced a lively debate among parents. But it was the response of children which interested Campbell most, as she reports 'children of reception age were discussing points of grammar and explaining to the teacher 'my Mum says it should be this way round" (Campbell, 2008).

A further development in dual language books emerged when teachers bid for funding for special projects that enabled them to formally publish work developed in schools.

The publication of dual language books
The Newham Women's Community Writing Group

This dual language book making project, run by Eve Gregory, was one of the earliest, right at the beginning of the 1980s. The black and white picture books that emerged from it were popular with teachers, widely used in London and beyond and enjoyed by children who often coloured in their personal copies. Loving stories and book making, Gregory explains the primary purpose of her project 'It made sense to me that children should have access to stories in their mother tongue' (Gregory, 2008a). Working in increasingly multilingual schools, she noticed that children who couldn't understand the story being read in class were bored. She invited parents to read stories to groups of children.

> What struck me then was that the children would come rushing back from having heard these stories ... really keen to share all of that with their teacher, but they couldn't, because their English wasn't good enough to translate it all.

So Gregory developed the idea of making the stories into dual language books. A grant from UNESCO for women's education projects enabled her to bring women together from a range of language backgrounds in the parents' room of a primary school. The women indicated they would like to tell stories from their own childhood. As the stories developed, they were translated into Urdu, Gujarati, Punjabi and English, and were illustrated by one of the women. Other stories were written and illustrated by secondary school children for younger children. The traditional stories from different cultures were grouped by themes, such as greed, or wishing. The aim was to produce sophisticated stories that could be written in an English that was accessible to children new to the language. The books were initially copied on duplicators, before a small publisher was found who produced them cheaply. They were widely distributed to schools by Gregory's own family, enabling the grant from UNESCO to be stretched further. Later a mainstream educational publisher took on the project and published the books commercially, but ceased publication some time later, claiming that there was insufficient demand.

Talking about the project, and the subsequent making of dual language resources in Newham, Gregory is nostalgic about the richness of the process of book making: the close relationships with mothers, the hidden talents discovered and shared, the learning for the whole school, children's pride and enthusiasm and the benefits in language and literacy development.

Local Education Authority publishing
Several Local Education Authorities (LEAs) supported the production of multicultural and multilingual materials. An example is Waltham Forest's Multicultural Development Service which funded the production of small dual language books in Urdu, Bengali and Punjabi, first published in 1982. The production was co-ordinated by John Welch who explains 'the drive to develop multiculturalism and raise awareness of languages' and the importance of ensuring the visible presence of the languages in school (John Welch, 2009). Used by all primary schools in the borough, the books were also available for sale and were widely distributed. The short stories, illustrated with line drawings in black and white, dealt with events in children's lives, such as *Naughty Imran* (Walker, 1984). The local authority built up a very substantial collection of dual language books throughout the 1980s and produced a valuable bibliography of available titles (Bahl, 1989).

Reading Materials for Minority Groups project
Some very popular and enduring dual language books were developed as part of a funded multilingual story telling project entitled Reading Materials for Minority Groups directed by Jennie Ingham from 1982 to 1985 and based at Middlesex Polytechnic. The project's primary purpose was a consideration of the importance of ... 'recognising and accepting the child's cultural background as legitimate and valid' (Ingham, 1986:2).

Like the Newham project, it aimed to encourage parents from minority linguistic communities to share their story telling traditions with children in primary schools. The children then used these stories as a basis for drama productions, art work, book making and cross curricular activities. Parents, teachers, story tellers, translators and illustrators worked collaboratively to prepare versions of the stories for publication. The funding (from the Cadmean Trust) enabled a range of these to be published in dual text versions in English and the languages most commonly spoken by children in local schools.

Like others described in this section, the project was rooted in collaborative story-telling at school level. However the involvement of experienced illustrators like Amanda Welch (who also illustrated the Waltham Forest books mentioned above) and the high quality colour printing produced books with commercial standard production values. Over twenty titles were eventually published and were instrumental in establishing that there could, after all, be a market for dual language story books for children.

Fourteen schools were involved in the north London area. As in the other projects, the process proved to be as valuable to the participants as the finished product. A headteacher commented on the benefits in terms of increased parental involvement in the school:

> ... where parents are genuinely needed, the effect on their attitude to the school can be very marked and will, in turn, affect their children's attitudes to school. (Ingham, 1986:3)

A parent drawn in by her child, who wanted her to come and read the story in Greek to his class, ended up becoming involved with the school on a regular basis. Accounts by teachers involved bear witness to the excitement of children when they first encounter a 'proper book' in their home language and how greatly they value it, wish to share it and 'begin to see books as friends' (*op cit*:2). The project provided some advice on the use of dual language books and, in particular, it suggested that 'In mainstream schools dual language books can be the ideal way of teaching a child to read English, whilst maintaining and reinforcing the mother tongue' (*op cit*:9).

As in similar school-based book-making projects, by the process of developing a traditional story collaboratively with children through a range of media, the story becomes transformed for its new audience of multilingual British schoolchildren. One of the best known stories to emerge from the Reading Materials for Minority Groups Project was the *Raja's Big Ears* (Desai, 1989). The journey it travelled from rural Gujarat to Inner London and its transformation at the hands of a storyteller working with local school children is described in Chapter 4.

Kurdish folktales

In the early 1990s a small collection of Kurdish folktales was produced in Hackney. Two colourful and eye-catching books were developed in Sorani and English and had an impact far beyond the Kurdish refugee community for whose children they were written. The stories appealed to children of all backgrounds and provided a starting point for story-telling, drama, and children's own interpretations of the story which they developed in their own writing as well as in artwork inspired by the powerful and intriguing illustrations.

The project was initiated by Hackney PACT (Parents and Children and Teachers) a project run from the Educational Psychology section of the Education Directorate to encourage parents to read at home with their children. The needs of bilingual children and parents were taken into account early on in the PACT project. Advice booklets, reading cards and tapes were produced in the languages most commonly spoken in the borough. Schools were advised to send home dual language books and encourage parents to read to their children in both the family language and English when possible (Hancock, 1995).

A grant from the Government's Inner City Partnership programme supported the project developed by Hancock. The aim was to produce versions of stories that parents from the refugee Kurdish community might tell to their children, to tap into families' oral traditions and to reflect them in well produced books that would be available in school libraries. Hancock describes how a Kurdish colleague hurried off to the Iranian part of Kurdistan to seek a small collection of stories from a famous, elderly and very frail story teller (2007). The stories brought back were hand-written in Sorani and included small line drawings. They were translated into English, then reworked by Edward Korel, a children's author, into a more dramatic, poetic and more western style of narrative. The stories were then translated back into Sorani. Kagan Güner, a Turkish artist, himself a refugee, was commissioned to illustrate the books, edited by Hancock and published by Learning by Design.

The three funded projects described so far have all started from the wish to value children's culture. Blackledge, in a study of home-school literacy practices in a Bangladeshi community in Birmingham, has commented on the value of dual language books when they reflect the culture and heritage of a particular community (2000). The books in Hancock's project were aimed precisely at valuing the culture of the many Kurdish refugees who arrived and settled in Hackney in the early 1990s. The project's aim was that children would pick up the book in the library, find that they could relate to the story, the artwork and the script and be proud to show it to other children.

As others have found when developing such projects, they provide a steep learning curve. Issues of language and identity are never simple and can bring with them the baggage of conflict. Hancock reflected, in an interview (2007), on some of the unexpected issues he was faced with and the learning that resulted for himself and for the production team. He concluded that far more can be learned from the collaborative process of colleagues working across cultures, than from many a textbook. For example, the reality of 'Kurdistan', a people without a nation, whose geographical situation covers several countries, whose language, culture and people are marginalised and persecuted, is a minefield for the uninitiated. 'Once you get into this, you suddenly realise you can be an innocent with regards to the politics and divisions. You can stumble into it, really,' commented Hancock when he discovered that some members of the refugee Kurdish community, from the Turkish side of the border, were uncomfortable with his choice of Sorani, from the Iranian side, for the stories.

With the same aim of providing folk tales that would be familiar to children, newly arrived as refugees, in a language they could understand, the Refugee Council published a series of stories in nine languages, in parallel volumes. The books also aimed to familiarise other children in the school with the language and culture of the newcomers. The stories are well chosen and the substantial amount of text makes them suitable for the more proficient reader. Each story has a map and information about its country of origin.

Bradford Partnership Publishing

The three books published by the Bradford project had different purposes. They were not aimed at newcomers but at children who were mostly born in Bradford to families from Pakistan. The book-making project was funded by the Kirklees Local Education Authority with the express purpose of valuing and promoting bilingualism in schools. The books were developed in different ways and are presented in different formats. The project was carried out by students on a course for bilingual teachers. Aimed at bilingual children in Bradford, all are in English and Urdu. The production process involved student teachers writing stories bilingually and then developing the narratives with children in the classroom.

The issue of directionality is an important one for dual language books written in English and Arabic or Urdu. An innovative and very attractive solution was found for *The Moving Mango Tree* (Jabeen, 1992), a collection of short stories for advanced readers, which is presented in a folder which can be opened from left to right for English or right to left for Urdu.

The other two texts also depart from the usual dual language book model. Unlike the commonly produced translated folk tales, they have the structure of contemporary children's stories, and reflect children's experiences of every-day life in Bradford. *The Balloon Detectives* (Jones, 1996) is presented in two volumes, each opening in the appropriate direction. An innovative addition is the transliterated text which has been added below the Urdu script. The use of transliteration is controversial as it clearly identifies the text as being viewed from an anglocentric perspective. However it can provide a valuable prop for the reader inexperienced in decoding the Urdu script. Jean Conteh (2008) describes how she was able, with some coaching from children, to use the transliterated text to read the story. She comments 'then the children would laugh and tell me how to say it properly!' *Send for Sohail* (Grange Road First School, 1993), developed with children in class, is based on a story struc-ture from the Ahlbergs. It addresses the issue of directionality in another innovative way: the book opens from bottom to top like a calendar. The books are expensively and elegantly produced, which was possible because they were designed and produced by the Arts and Textile Department of Bradford College.

Commercial publication

The majority of early published bilingual books were not commercial ventures. They were developed through special projects and publication was subsidised by project grants. However as their popularity grew and publishers became aware that sticky-label translations were being applied to their texts, translated versions of popular children's picture books were published in a range of languages. The bibliography produced by the Waltham Forest Multi-cultural Service gives some idea of the range of publishers making books available in dual language format. Bahl lists 21 publishers and includes both subsidised projects and mainstream publishers. The books listed include the usual folk tales, many specially written stories that portray the everyday life of children in a multicultural environment and some non-fiction titles. Some mainstream publishers made available popular stories such as Eric Hill's *Spot* series in dual text format. By far the most commonly available languages were South Asian (Urdu, Bengali, Punjabi and Gujarati), but the bibliography lists titles available in 22 languages.

The dual language book market was not sufficiently lucrative to retain the attention of many mainstream publishers. Books published by the Chicago-based Milet are available in the UK in 26 languages and include contemporary stories alongside some folk tales from a range of cultures. Currently the most widely known publisher in the UK, Mantra Lingua, started as a small family company in 1984 producing contemporary multicultural and dual language books in four South Asian languages. It currently publishes in fifty languages with eighty titles in print. It is known internationally and has major business in the US. As well as translations of popular texts (such as *Dear Zoo, Brown Bear, Brown Bear, what do you see?*), traditional folk tales, such as *The Giant Turnip* or *The Musicians of Bremen*, have been reinvented for multilingual publication. Attractively published stories originating from different countries round the world have been commissioned. Commercial viability is achieved through meeting the demand for the publication of the same folk tale in a wide range of languages from schools that use them as core texts to teach reading and create a shared literary culture in their classrooms. Many of the dual language texts used by the children in the present study were Mantra publications. The Redbridge project, in which the teachers who taught Magda, Albana, Mohammed, Sarah, Lek and Durkan were involved, ordered in bulk from Mantra the dual language books that it provided to all the primary schools in the authority.

The books are well written and illustrated and have high production values. They were very popular with the children in the present study as they provided interesting reading material in the language of the home. However, not all children will recognise themselves and their culture in the books. Much as Magda and Albana loved the stories (and they devoured most of what has been published in Albanian) not a single one reflected life in Albania or told an Albanian folk tale. Lek and Durkan would also have welcomed a Turkish story.

Developments in the 21st Century

The tradition of sharing resources that started with circulating translations on duplicated sheets and labels and copied tapes in Teachers' Centres has come of age with the availability of new software and the internet. Many schools and local authorities, such as Hounslow, are making dual language books and related multilingual resources developed by teachers freely available to colleagues on their websites. The availability of affordable digital cameras, digital sound and video recording, multilingual word processing and software that provides book-making templates (such as Clicker 5) has revolutionised the production of books. The process is very much easier than it was 30 years ago and children are able to produce professional looking books. The main developments in multilingual materials from commercial publishers have followed the same trend. Advances in technology in the early 1990s enabled Mantra Lingua to greatly increase the number of languages in which it could publish and drove their large scale development of CD-ROMs. However, alongside the audio CD, the interactive DVD and the online talking books, the traditional paper book continues to be popular and small independent publishers are creating new books for a specific purpose with a particular audience in mind.

Multimedia productions

The Fabula project was developed to provide a multimedia authoring tool to make dual language books in minority European languages such as Basque and Welsh. The project provides some of the best recent examples of children working collaboratively to write, translate and illustrate their own stories. It demonstrates how much learning about the process of translation and parallel authoring develops children's awareness of language and how 'The active involvement of children as collaborative creators rather than consumers is central to the successful use of software in classrooms' (Edwards *et al*, 2002:60).

A good example of a site that makes high quality multilingual material available free or for a modest charge is the Hounslow Virtual Education Centre. The traditional story of the *Man, the Boy and the Donkey* (Carter, 2007) is freely available on the site as a talking book, in English and eight other languages. Each page has an illustration and two boxes with text, the first in English, the second in one of the other languages. There are buttons to click to hear the sound in both languages on the page. The stories can be used in many different ways with children: projected for use with a whole class, on an individual computer for use by individuals or groups of children, in printed format to read in a book corner or to take home. The texts can help children who are readers in their first language to support learning to read in English and can also be used the other way round. Additional stories in the same format can be purchased on DVD. Particularly interesting is the availability of a version in British Sign Language: at the click of the mouse a television screen appears with a signer who interprets the page of text written in English.

The Clicker software used for these stories has been widely promoted to schools as a means of making dual language books and teachers have been trained to use it in workshops organised by the company. It provides templates which enables teachers to work with children to produce their own stories and record their own text. These are ideal resources to use in family learning or story making workshops with parents and children as well as in the classroom.

Another example of dual language stories available on DVD is published by Espresso Primary. Three stories, including a perennial favourite, *The Six Blind Men and the Elephant* (Carter and Ahmed, 2007), come in Arabic, English, Bengali, Urdu and Somali. Like the Clicker resources they can be used in many ways in the classroom and include interactive whiteboard resources and a talking dictionary. They are accompanied by a wide range of resources for related activities. In a sequence *From Story to Play* children explain, step by step, how to turn a traditional Somali story in dual language text into a play, culminating in a confident and delightful performance.

It is clear from the way in which these resources are produced that they are intended to be used for a wide range of purposes and, in particular, to stimulate children to produce their own writing and make their own multimedia, multilingual materials. Both sets of resources mentioned above also make reference to their value in engaging with parents and the community.

It is possible to explore the internet and find many other examples of dual language stories that can be freely downloaded from sites around the world. The collection of stories available from the BBC education site, Around the World at Cbeebies (2008), is designed to introduce children to famous traditional stories in their original language. The story of *Babushka* is told in Russian, the *Hodja* in Turkish. The stories are available in thirteen languages and can be projected for a whole class or downloaded and printed. However, while they fulfill the object of providing genuine stories from a particular culture, the texts are not so useful for reading as dual language books: the original language of the story is printed at the bottom of each page as part of the image and a translation in English is available at the side. This raises the issue of parity of text as, although the original language seems to be promoted as more significant, it is not always clearly legible and blurs when enlarged. Unlike the other resources referred to above, the books do not have an audio file.

In its drive to make full use of new technology to make languages accessible and books interactive, Mantra Lingua developed the Talking Pen and its later incarnation, the Recorder Pen. The pen operates as an MP3 player that can store text for specified books in a range of languages. Once the text and language have been chosen, the pen will read each page of a book when pointed at a microdot at the corner of a page. The pen's great advantage is its mobility: it does not require a computer, can be used by an individual or a group of children anywhere in the classroom, can be sent home with a book, or can be used quietly with headphones. Unlike a CD based talking book, it accompanies a real book that can be used in the conventional way (Pim, 2008). Its ease of use makes it accessible to very young children. It provides support for children learning to read in either English or the language of the home.

The Recorder Pen offers new access to curriculum resources. While it is generally used in conjunction with dual language books, the pen can be used to provide an audio file in any language for use with English only materials. While this makes it more economical for a school, it is less useful for children who are learning to read in their first language and it does not contribute to a multilingual print environment.

The Recorder Pen works in a similar way to the Talking Pen, but has the added advantage that teachers, parents and children can record material linked directly to words on the page, either through the use of small stickers which act as hot spots or through purpose made books. For example parents can personalise their recording of a story to match their own child's understanding: expanding, explaining, using more accessible words. As the stickers can be put anywhere, children's own writing as well as material all around the classroom can be recorded and played at the touch of the pen. Published resources for the Recorder Pen include some materials in Sylheti, the language spoken in the home by the majority of families of Bangladeshi origin in Britain, as well as in standard Bengali, thus adding flexibility to the issue of language choice for translation.

The award-winning Language of the Month site, created by Joe Debono at Newbury Park Primary School, has been made available free since its beginning in 2002. For each language spoken in the school, the site has information, obtained by working with parents and children, about where the language is spoken and a range of resources and games that can be printed as a pack for teachers. One of the most attractive features of the programme is the section in which one can click on a word, phrase, or number and see a child from the school demonstrating the pronunciation (Debono, 2002). There are currently materials in 43 languages on the site. It has inspired many teachers to use its resources when making dual language books, and also to adapt its principles to the needs of different groups of children, as Mullis did for children in the Foundation Stage (2007).

Small scale publication

While all the multimedia resources mentioned above are valuable for use in the classroom, they do not replace a well produced book. A book is not dependent on technology being available in the home and it can be shared anywhere, with anyone.

An interesting development in the publication of dual language books is the tiny publisher creating a book for a specific purpose and a specific audience. This is generally a venture organised by one individual or family. Typically one book is produced to test responses, with the aim of following it up if it proves successful. One book produced in this way is *The Fisherman and the Cat* (Ashraf, 2007). An original story in English and Gujarati set in the Arabian sea, it is accompanied by an audio CD. The book is aimed at second and third generation Gujarati speakers who regret that they are not fluent or literate in the language of their family. The publisher explains:

> I searched for bilingual storybooks to support my language learning attempts. I wanted to try hard, to find the one thing I knew I needed to bridge my two worlds. I knew exactly how it should look and feel, but it was nowhere to be found. (Ashraf, 2008)

So she wrote and published the book she couldn't find. While it is attractively illustrated, the book does not look like a children's picture book and is suitable for both adults and children. As well as text in both Gujarati and English, the learner is supported by a transliteration of the Gujarati into Roman script, and by teaching notes on the Gujarati script and on key vocabulary.

Another example is *Ceren's Love of Books* (Asan, 2007), published in Turkish and English. Aimed specifically at encouraging Turkish families to read to their children, the story shows how the mother of a young girl uses books, storytelling and rhymes to enhance her daughter's everyday experiences.

Responses to the language teaching agenda

Other publishers are developing materials to meet the demands of the language teaching curriculum in primary schools. *Où es-tu Petit Loup?* (Synek, 2008), is accompanied by lesson plans and extension activities freely available on the publisher's website and was produced by Bramhall, a publisher dissatisfied with available dual language books for teaching French to young children.

The development of language teaching in primary schools as a result of the Key Stage 2 *Framework for Languages* (DfES, 2005) has led to a strong development in resources, although these have been mainly in the more traditional European modern languages. In the same way as teachers who taught English as an additional language to bilingual children in the seventies and early eighties, teachers of languages are now developing their own resources and games and, in the same spirit, are making them available to colleagues. The main difference being that, instead of swapping sticky labels, they are swapping internet references. Or so I thought, until I came across messages on a network for language teachers that indicated that teachers were, once again, producing their own translations of popular picture books and even, in one case, putting them on sticky labels.

Long standing publishers of dual language books, like Mantra, have greatly extended their range of materials to meet this new demand. Other language teaching publishers have developed resources, some of them in dual language format with a full complement of classroom resources, such as lesson plans and interactive whiteboard resources. While teachers of languages in the primary school swap notes and recommendations on professional networks, action research projects set up to evaluate the use and value of the new resources in the classroom would be welcome.

Research and evaluation

While the writing and production of dual language books was developing in multilingual schools, comparatively little was written about the books or their use. In the 1980s the ILEA was introducing bilingual development in selected schools, supported by a team of community language teachers. Ming Tsow, the inspector for community languages who led the team, noted that publishers and individuals seeking ready made markets had also started producing dual language (parallel language) texts, to capitalise on the dearth of suitable materials (1986:13). However, she expressed concern that materials were being produced in the absence of any research on the use of dual language text or on the process of reading simultaneously in two languages.

Ming Tsow carried out a small observational study of developing bilinguals who had access to teachers of community languages in their mainstream primary schools. The teachers observed children reading *Where's Spot* (Hill, 1984) in Bengali/English and Chinese/English versions. They also used a Greek stand-alone translation of the text (as no dual language version was available). The study demonstrates a range of strategies used by children whose language variety, in all three languages, was very different from the standard used in the books. Ming-Tsow notes that the experiences of reading were very positive, that children were highly motivated and she commented on their excitement and tenacity. A similarly high level of motivation is a striking feature of the children in the present study, as reported in the later chapters of this book. It is particularly interesting to find, twenty years on, that the issues remain much the same and that children encountering the books with skilled adult support respond with the same enthusiasm, motivation and a broad range of strategies to make meaning across the languages.

The most comprehensive discussion of the nature and use of dual language books in the English education system since the early 1980s can be found in a book which provides guidance for teachers on a range of resources designed to encourage the use of languages other than English in the classroom. The views of children and teachers were sought regarding different materials and their use in an action research project based at the University of Reading, The Multilingual Resources for Children Project (MRC, 1995), directed by Viv Edwards and Sarah Walker.

Teachers consulted noted that, whereas books in a single language could only really be used by readers of that language, dual language books were accessible to a much wider range of pupils. Teachers using dual language texts can confidently discuss the story with children. This use has been noted by Gravelle (1996) as possibly the main benefit of the books. Examples of this are to be found in the Redbridge Project mentioned above and in the classrooms of the children who feature in the case studies in this volume. Teachers also reported feeling confident about using them for raising awareness of languages, for encouraging children to explore an unfamiliar script and make hypotheses, thereby revealing a great deal about what they know (and don't know) about how language works. Use of the books encourages children to share their languages, thereby promoting pride in language skills and cultural identity.

Children interviewed for the Reading project who used the books shared these views and were particularly aware of the positive effect their presence in the classroom would have on children new to English faced with unfamiliar classroom materials. They also especially liked the fact that one language could act as a prop for another: 'you can learn quicker than if there's just one language' (1995:56).Teachers reported that children new to English who were literate in their first language could use the books to support their understanding of the English text and to help them develop new vocabulary.

Teachers also noted that the books were popular with parents and acted as 'a bridge between home and school', encouraging parents to read with children in their home language (1995:54). This aspect was confirmed in the present case studies, in which all parents participating were keen on the books sent home by the school as they had difficulty in obtaining any other kind of children's books in their language.

However, the use of books with two different texts on the page was not uniformly popular with the Reading teachers. Some teachers in mainstream schools, but most particularly those who worked in complementary schools, expressed a concern that children who were dominant in English would just read the much easier (for them) text in English and not engage with the other language.

The MRC report has an extensive section that addresses issues of design illustrated with examples of dual language books of different types, including many of those developed by projects described in this chapter. The lay out chosen, the respective position of the two texts and the illustrations, typography and directionality of the book, all of these raise issues of the status of the languages on the page. Children consulted demonstrated a keen awareness of such issues and had a great deal to say about layout, font and the general attractiveness and readability of text. The innovative design of the Bradford books addressed the issue of the different directionality of Urdu and English, producing books in which both languages have equal status.

More recent research includes the observational case study of a recently arrived Chinese speaking child reading dual language books. It shows the child and her mother collaborating on the task of reading together and demonstrates the role of shared cultural knowledge in the learning process. Through the use of the books, the mother, who is not literate in English, is able to support her child's reading in English as well as developing her knowledge of Chinese. Ma stresses how, as found in the study of Magda and Albana, the books enable the mother to become much more involved with her child's education, as well as improving her own knowledge of English: 'the mother helps her child to learn and learns from the child' (Ma, 2008:10).

A dual language book also features in a study by Robertson (2006) of five young Pahari speaking children learning to read in Urdu. While not making use of dual language texts, a recent project in Tower Hamlets explores how children study texts and carry out activities using both Bengali and English in their mainstream classrooms (Kenner *et al*, 2008a). Both these studies are discussed in Chapter 2.

Action Research

The Multilingual Resources for Children Project demonstrated the value of teachers working together to experiment with and evaluate new resources. The very much smaller Action Research Project based at UEL was designed to support a new generation of teachers in exploring the use of multilingual materials in their classroom. The teachers met regularly over a period of two years, tried out and assessed the impact of new ideas, shared problems, helped each other with solutions and generally shared information. A particular feature of the project was the involvement of the Mantra publishing company who was keen to know how their materials were used in the classroom and what additional resources teachers would like. The teachers' ideas have been published on websites (Sneddon, 2007; Mullis, 2007; Kabra, 2007) and some of the games they designed in class were developed and published by Mantra.

With a similar intent, the Redbridge project Developing Reading Skills through Home Languages (EMAT, 2008), co-ordinated by Samina Jaffar, aimed to create a reading culture in the home language that would complement and support children's learning to read in school in English. The project provided dual language books to primary schools in the borough. It set up a working party of six teachers who promoted them in the classroom and supported parents in using them in the home. Using action research methods, the teachers developed a range of multilingual resources which were published at the end of the project.

The work of the teachers involved in the last two of these projects inspired the present study and provided access to the families of the children who feature in the case studies.

Reservations and controversies

Researchers and practitioners acknowledge that the use of dual language books is controversial. Edwards, who has extensive experience of multilingual material development, stresses the positive aspects of their use:

> ...dual texts represent a very valuable way of keeping other languages in high profile; they also offer opportunities for teachers to encourage children's biliterate development. (1998:61)

Others have reservations. Many of these were addressed in the MRC project and centre around two key issues: whether it is a good idea in principle to have two texts on a page; and specific issues that arise from individual stories.

Whatever the production standards and the status of the two languages in an individual book, the fact that all the dual language books in a classroom include English clearly identifies it as the default language, the dominant language of the curriculum and the language through which all others are viewed. The texts chosen for production are chosen because they are suitable for bridging languages and cultures and are, in many cases, chosen by English teachers and publishers. This is in contrast with books imported from countries of origin, which will reflect the children's literature and the culture of that country. As discussed in the section on translation, it is common for many books, including children's, in multilingual countries such as India, to be published separately in several languages, including English.

A dual language book provides a prop for the less proficient reader. It is less time-consuming than using a dictionary, an intrusive procedure than can lead the reader to lose the flow and meaning of the text. Reading a stand alone text in the target language is the best strategy to develop fully the skills of a more advanced learner. However, more advanced readers have also been known to value literature in translation in dual language format as it can provide access to difficult classics in a less well known language and offers an opportunity to reflect on shades of meaning and alternative interpretations.

While recognising the value of dual language books, several authors have been concerned that they are often the only resource in languages other than English in the classroom. If the aim is to value children's home languages, Gravelle considers that children and their parents may well prefer to have access to 'a good range of books written in the first language... alongside the English books' (1996:59). She doubts whether a translated text, which will inevitably differ in detail from the original, really supports learning to read a language. She is also concerned that, because most dual language books are picture books for younger children, with few non-fiction books or books for older children available, this might create a distorted image of what is available in different languages (1996:60). She raises similar concerns to those addressed in the MRC project regarding the size, position and directionality of print and the implications these have for language status.

Gravelle acknowledges that dual language books have a place in the classroom if parents find them useful. In a later publication she has demonstrated how a dual language book can act as a powerful stimulus for children to write their own books in two languages (Gravelle, 2000).

Kenner is a strong advocate of creating a multilingual environment in the classroom. However, while she acknowledges the value of using dual language books, she considers them to represent very much a school model of literacy. She is keen for children to bring materials from home that are culturally appropriate, reflect familiar literacy events and bridge the home-school gap from the perspective of the home (Kenner, 2000a:17).

There is a strong argument for schools that are serious about encouraging children to learn languages to have a small library of books in those languages. I have personal experience of creating such a collection in a primary school in 1984, with the help of parents and teachers from complementary schools. I was not alone in this and regularly swapped notes with colleagues about the best book shops. Such a collection would be ideal for children like Albana, Magda and especially Sarah, who have outgrown all the dual language picture books available in Albanian and in French and are keen to develop their reading skills further with more authentic material. The limited resources available to schools for book buying make it unlikely that schools would invest in this option. It is more viable in secondary schools in which the languages are taught to examination level. In the 1980s and 1990s many teachers' centres had resource collections which they would lend to schools and these often included books in community languages. It is unfortunate that, with more funding now devolved directly to schools, many of the collections, such as the extensive one in Waltham Forest, have been mothballed or disbanded.

An important issue raised by Blackledge is not so much about the books themselves but the context in which they are used, in particular with respect to the relationship between home and school. He comments that dual language books can only be deployed effectively in the context of a school that has good relationships with parents and knows which languages and language varieties they speak. Teachers also need to know in which languages family members are literate. Blackledge also stresses that teachers need to provide advice and support for parents so that they know what is expected of them. As well as knowing about families' home languages, he suggests that schools need to be responsive to parents' needs. He is also concerned that

> The best dual language text books are often written from the perspective of the home culture and translated into English, rather than vice-versa, making them more culturally relevant ... (2000:86)

Such texts will help children to feel that their personal experience is recognised and valued. This has been the primary purpose of many of the books produced through specific projects: Gregory, Hancock and Ingham, John and Baker all aimed to publish books that brought children's culture and experience into the classroom.

The available research, while limited, has generally been positive about the value of dual language books in raising the profile of languages in the classroom. All who have created or used the books with families have found that they were generally welcome. The motivation mentioned for many of the book making projects was to value children's cultural heritage, of which language is a part. All those who developed and published the books reported a considerable benefit that resulted to children from the much greater involvement of parents and the community as experts in the school. However the only study so far that provides hard evidence of the benefits in terms of language learning is that of James Ma.

The reservations expressed about the use of the books raise important issues for teachers. Blackledge has concerns about teachers' knowledge of the language and literacy of the community; Hancock has admitted his naivety with respect to the politics of Kurdish. Kenner and Gravelle are concerned that books, now readily available in a wide range of languages, may replace the creative use of more authentic materials that reflect the literacy practices of a community.

Clark *et al* (1990) have raised concerns about naïve and uncritical approaches to language awareness in schools which fail to take account of ideological struggles and power relations. This has also been raised by Harris in his challenge of what he calls 'romantic bilingualism' (Harris, 1997). Weight is lent to his comments by the considerable anecdotal evidence of teachers purchasing dual language books and then not really knowing how to use them.

The answer may be that teachers need opportunities to develop a greater awareness of the complexity of the multilingualism and multiliteracy in their community, and be prepared to engage with the learning curve described by Hancock. By engaging in dialogue with bilingual parents and colleagues on issues such as those mentioned by Colledge and Campbell, they will learn a great deal about the value and limitations of translation and become more confident about experimenting in the use of multilingual materials in school.

They especially need to be aware of the perception of the value of languages in the wider society to understand why the same little girl, mentioned at the beginning of this chapter, who is so enthusiastic about having a book in her own language, may, later in her schooling, ask, like Medmedbegovic's respondent 'Miss, who needs the language of immigrants?'.

Conclusion

This chapter has described some of the ways in which dual language books have been developed and used with children in the classroom. Most of the benefits of using the books, as well as some of the drawbacks, were identified many years ago by the teachers involved in the Multilingual Resources for Children project. The evidence it provided, as well as advances in technology, raised standards of production.

Researchers and practitioners have identified drawbacks in the concept of the books as well as problems generated by their uncritical use. However, what also emerges is how enriching the process of working with the books, whether choosing them and planning activities or the actual process of making them, has proved to be. Teachers who have worked collaboratively with children, parents, storytellers, writers and artists to produce books, have all commented on how much they gained from the process. The books provide an opportunity to engage the creativity of all concerned and take them on a learning journey: Roger Hancock reflected on his new understanding of language politics; Amanda Welch, remembering her work on the Jennie Ingham books: 'It was such *fun!*'

Buying the books and putting them in the school or class library, like displaying a multilingual welcome poster, is not enough to guarantee that languages are valued and used in school. The future of dual language books lies in their recognition and use as an important tool for language learning and the valuing of personal experience and identity. Used critically for specific purposes in conjunction with other language resources, they can greatly enrich the curriculum. Advances in audio and visual media technologies extend the use and value of the books in the class and in the home. New developments in software and hardware open up new opportunities and ways of exploring languages. The internet provides opportunities for collaborating and sharing across schools and countries.

The *Every Child Matters* policy (DfES, 2005), the different strands of the curriculum for languages and literacy and developments in ICT and multimedia technology empower teachers to enable children to continue to explore their personal experience to make books that they will treasure.

Keya Ashraf explains how much bilingual books mean to her:

> Bilingual books are more than simply texts in two languages, more than nursery rhymes and numbers in different fonts. Until academics and establishment figures understand this, languages will continue to come under threat.

Those who go through the sad experience of losing a language know that the feeling of language lives on long after the last words are ever spoken. Bilingual books ignite the feelings and thoughts belonging to language – in one world, two languages. (Ashraf, 2008)

2
Language use and literacy practices in families and communities

This chapter explores the language context in which dual language books are used in British schools. In most instances teachers, who have made or used them have done so in response to a perceived need in their classrooms. As the previous chapter shows, finding out about children's languages, making and choosing resources and encouraging children's literacy in a range of languages has always required a close engagement with the children's families. For many teachers this engagement with families and the wider community and the impact on children's achievement has proved to be one of the greatest and most enduring benefits of using multilingual resources.

The chapter provides some examples of the linguistic context in which many teachers operate. It explores some definitions of bilingualism, current policies and the contribution of recent research to understanding the benefits and challenges of bilingualism, how children become multiliterate and the role that families and communities play in this process.

The language context
Since the 1960s the population of bilingual children has risen substantially. The first children arriving in Britain from overseas came primarily from Commonwealth countries and the languages they spoke reflected this. Families settled where work was available and formed supportive networks in areas of affordable housing.

The languages in which books were produced reflect the local priorities of the teachers who developed them. Jennie Ingham produced books in Greek, Turkish, Urdu, Hindi, Punjabi, Bengali and Gujarati, those being the main languages spoken by children in London schools at the time. Jean Conteh's books, on the other hand, were all developed in Urdu as the vast majority of the new population of Bradford originated from Pakistan. Roger Hancock focused on Kurdish, to meet the needs of the substantial population of Turkish refugees who settled in Hackney in east London. Janet Campbell's books were targeted at the many Turkish children who lived in north east London where she taught.

The most comprehensive survey of the languages spoken by children in any area is to be found in Multilingual Capital (Baker and Eversley, 2000) which maps, borough by borough, the 300 languages spoken by children in the capital. But since this book was published, civil wars, conflicts and the widening of the European Union have greatly increased, not only the overall numbers of bilingual children entering school, but the range of languages spoken (Somali, Albanian, Polish, Czech, Lithuanian, Latvian etc).

The patterns of community settlement determine the language make-up of any particular neighbourhood school. Depending on the nature of their economic activity and their particular religious, cultural or dietary needs, some communities stay close together, like the Bangladeshi community in Tower Hamlets, and develop their own neighbourhood services. Other communities, like the Chinese, disperse (Li Wei, 1994). So certain schools may have large proportions of bilingual children speaking mainly one language while others will have 40 or more languages spoken in a single primary school and upwards of 80 in secondary schools. For teachers wishing to value and support children's community languages, the challenges presented by these situations are considerable.

How bilingual is bilingual?
Most of the books described so far were developed for use with bilingual children. So who exactly is bilingual? While more than half the population of the world is bi- or multilingual, in essentially monolingual societies it is not uncommon to consider that one is only bilingual if one is equally proficient in two or more languages. This form of 'balanced bilingualism' is comparatively rare, as most bilinguals have developed a range of languages for use in different domains.

In a study of young bilingual children's developing literacy, Bialystok engages with the complex matter of defining bilingualism. She notes that bilingualism is a continuum, from the essentially monolingual child who has learned a few words in another language, to the child who is proficient and literate in two languages. Any definition raises issues of language proficiency which is notoriously difficult to measure. It also raises the issue of how one defines a language: what about the child who speaks what is defined as a dialect, but may be unintelligible to a speaker of the standard language? (Bialystok, 2001)

In recognition of the complexity of these issues and the huge variety of patterns of language use within families who 'live in two languages', the definition provided by the DfES sidesteps these issues and offers the widest possible definition of bilingualism:

> Bilingual learners: all children who have access to more than one language at home or at school. It does not necessarily imply full fluency in both or all languages. *Aiming High: Raising the Achievement of Minority Ethnic Pupils* (DfES, 2003:28)

Many of these will be 'beginner bilinguals': children who have just arrived at school, speaking another language in the home and new to English. They are generally referred to as 'bilingual' in recognition of the fact that they commonly make rapid progress in conversational English in the school environment. Gregory prefers to use the term 'new language learner' to acknowledge that the acquisition of a new language doesn't just happen, but requires a substantial learning journey (Gregory, 2008b). Children who are learning English in school are referred to as learners of 'English as an additional language' in recognition of the multilingualism of children who have come from, for example, South Asian or African societies in which it is expected that people will speak (and often be literate in) local, regional and national languages; others may come from linguistically mixed families or have been resident and schooled in another European country before settling in Britain.

Teachers commonly ask children 'what language do you speak at home?' This apparently simple question can reveal complex and fascinating situations.

Both Harris (1997) and Blackledge (2000) have warned about the pitfalls of sending translated letters or dual language books home with children without having an accurate knowledge of what languages are actually in use in a child's family. What languages are used for and by whom will determine the pattern of language use that a child experiences in the home.

Where a child was born and brought up and how long a family has lived in the UK will also determine patterns of language use, maintenance and shift. Fishman has described (1980) a three generation pattern observed more recently by Li Wei (1994) in his work in the Chinese community, by which a family language can be lost within three generations in an immigrant community.

A common feature of bilingual speech is the use of various forms of code-mixing and switching. Bilinguals who meet regularly in the same language groups switch regularly, sometimes depending on the topic of conversation, sometimes even in mid-sentence or mid-word and this mixed code can become the norm for informal communication in many families and communities (Chana and Romaine, 1984).

An additive bilingual has added one language to another, for example English to Albanian, and eventually becomes proficient in both. However, language shift can be very rapid in situations in which the first language is not greatly valued or used in the community. Children then become subtractive bilinguals, losing the use of their first language as they acquire the second (Hamers and Blanc, 1989)

This has been a source of considerably anxiety for several of the parents who participated in the present study. Magda and Albana's parents arrived from Albania in 2000, educated in Albanian, and started to learn English as they made a new life in London. Their daughters, born in Britain, learned basic communicative English rapidly once they started school and, while they clearly understood their parents' Albanian, were becoming reluctant to use the language. This asymmetrical use of language is common and caused their families great concern.

Mydda was also born in England to a family in which the mother speaks Urdu and the father Punjabi. While both parents understand each other's language, communication within the family is complex and Mydda has become heavily dominant in English, her understanding of both Urdu and Punjabi being limited to basic communication and a fairly narrow vocabulary range in Urdu, the language which her family would most like her to learn.

How bilingual are the children in the present study? All understand the language of the home to varying extents. All can use the language but often choose not to. Sarah is the only one who is close to being a balanced bilingual. While her understanding and use of Lingala is fairly limited, her skills in both English and French are comparable in understanding, speaking and in reading. As an advanced reader in both languages her vocabulary range is wide as is her understanding of book language and metaphor. It is only in writing that her English is heavily dominant. She is an enthusiastic and experienced writer of stories in English but struggles greatly with spelling in French, having had virtually no experience of writing in that language.

How, then, do we find out how children use their languages? In the course of a study of the Gujarati and Urdu speaking community in north east London, trilingual children aged 7 and 11 were asked about their language use in a range of domains and with key people in their lives (Sneddon, 2000). A group of children aged 11 decided to interpret visually some of the key research questions and came up with the following diagram. I have used this with many children as a means of encouraging them to explore their own language use. As bilinguals know, they are often not aware of what language they are speaking at any given time.

The diagram shows how Mydda represents what she speaks to whom in her family. It indicates that, whereas her mother speaks more Urdu to her than English, Mydda responds mainly in English. Her father addresses her partly in Punjabi and partly in English, with Mydda responding trilingually, but mainly in English. All conversation with her older brother is in English, while her younger brother, who is not yet at school, speaks Urdu and Mydda responds to him primarily in English.

Activity sheet:
What languages do you speak with your family?

Key:

Colour	Language
	English
	puNjaBi
	Urdu

Mydda's language use in her family

31

Children enjoy the kind of discussion promoted by this analysis and many comment on how it makes them aware of patterns of language use that they do not normally notice. Teachers who have worked to develop children's languages in the classroom know the impact that exploring this issue with them has on children's confidence and pride in their linguistic skills.

The advantages and challenges of bilingualism

While the policies referred to in the introduction are generally positive with respect to bilingualism, the gap between policy and practice remains large. The implementation of the *National Languages Strategy* has revealed that many teachers are concerned about their lack of understanding of young children's language and literacy development, whether in relation to first language, English as an additional language, bilingualism or new language learning. The links between the different pedagogies involved in these aspects of language learning have barely begun to be explored (Conteh, 2008).

Much of the international research that demonstrates the benefits of bilingualism has been based on studying the achievement of pupils with access to different forms of bilingual education (Thomas and Collier, 2002; Cummins, 1996; Baker, 2006). There has been little research in this area in the UK and there is little bilingual education available outside Wales. The National Centre for Languages' *Positively Plurilingual* provides a brief summary of small-scale UK based studies and outlines the benefit of bilingualism as a linguistic, educational, intellectual, cultural and personal, as well as economic, resource. It suggests 'rather than thinking in terms of an 'English-only' culture, we should be promoting 'English plus" (CILT, 2007: 3).

However, recognition of the advantages of bilingualism, in the absence of any policies to actively promote it in mainstream education, does little to diminish the challenges faced by emergent bilinguals, or 'new language learners', as Gregory calls them, who are faced with learning to be literate in an additional, unfamiliar language. Many of these children have found their existing language skills ignored (Edwards, 2009) and their families may still be advised to focus only on the learning of English (Conteh *et al*, 2007). This contrasts with attitudes to the bilingualism of children who speak major European languages. International schools and European schools are popular with parents as their multilingual models of education ensure that children learn languages much more effectively than through the traditional secondary school model. The present study, like the early work on dual language books, has developed around three key areas of recent and current research: the transfer of concepts and skills across languages, multiliteracy, and partnerships between schools, families and communities.

The politics of language diversity, the status of individual languages in society and concepts of social justice are central to the theoretical framework developed by Cummins to explore the nature and impact of bilingualism (Cummins, 2000). A key element of Cummins' framework is the concept of the Common Underlying Proficiency (CUP) which explains how the cognitive skills associated with language operate from a central function and transfer between languages. There is considerable evidence for this and, in particular, for the fact that reading skills acquired in one language transfer readily, even when scripts are different (Cummins, 1984; Cummins, 1991; Cummins *et al*, 1984). It has been a common experience of teachers to find children new to English and literate in their first language making rapid progress in reading in English. Conversely, the children who are the focus of the present study, while they had all learned English as a second language, had become literate in English first. They were working to transfer skills learned in English to the language of the home.

The work of Bialystok on early bilingualism and literacy explores this kind of transfer of skills. Key concepts for young children to establish in relation to reading are phonological awareness (for languages that use an alphabetical principle) and an understanding of symbolic representation (Bialystock, 1997). She explores the complexity of the transfer of reading skills:

> Each language bears a slightly different relation to its printed form, each writing system represents the spoken language in a somewhat different manner, each social group places a different premium on literacy and provides different levels of access to it, and each educational system resolves the pedagogical issues independently. (Bialystok, 2004)

Bialystok notes that '... bilingual children have a more complete understanding of the symbolic relation between print and meaning than monolinguals' (2004:164), but of particular relevance to the present study is her finding that a difference in script between two languages doubles the difficulty of transferring skills. With reference to children who speak a minority language in the home, she also notes the particular difficulty they may have in learning to read in their weakest language.

> For children whose experience with literacy is in only one of the languages, it is probably the case that this experience is presented through the weaker of the two and not the language of the home. This is the language in which children

may be at greatest risk for possessing inadequate grammatical knowledge and insufficient background concepts of literacy, print, and text. (Bialystok, 2004:180)

The choice of languages in the case studies was designed to explore some of this complexity and how the differences between the pairs of languages impact on reading. It aimed to show how the children applied the skills that they had learned in English to read in languages that had different structures, different writing systems and different scripts: French, Turkish, Albanian, Urdu and Gujarati. English and French are Indo-European languages with a comparatively close relationship, as a good many words in the vocabulary of academic English originate from French and common sources in Latin and Greek. Turkish is not Indo-European and, as an agglutivative language, has a wholly different morphological and grammatical structure from English, with few common words, other than loan words. Albanian is Indo-European but in a class of its own and it also has a substantially different structure from English. All three of these languages are based on alphabetical principles and share with English the Roman alphabet. Edwards has noted the advantage that this represents as it enables an easier transfer of skills (Edwards, 1998). While sharing an alphabet and script is undeniably helpful, English differs from many alphabetic languages in its complex syllable structure and inconsistent spelling system (Wyse and Goswami, 2009) making it a more difficult language to learn to read than, for example, Turkish or Albanian.

Urdu and Gujarati present different challenges. Both are Indo-European languages and children who have explored languages with their teachers immediately notice similarities such as the fact that 'my name' in Gujarati is *maru nam*. But they have totally different scripts and, as Bialystok noted, this doubles the difficulty. Gujarati is based on the Devanagari script and written left to right, and Urdu is based on the Perso-Arabic script and written right to left. In addition to those differences the writing system is syllabic for Gujarati and consonantal for Urdu which affects the way vowels are represented in relation to consonants. An additional difficulty, that Mydda struggled with, is the fact that Urdu, like Arabic, has three different forms for each letter depending on whether it is initial, final or medial within a word.

As well as providing an explanation for different patterns of achievement among bilinguals in different contexts, Cummins' research also suggests how challenges can be turned to advantages and minority pupils empowered. While there is considerable evidence that a bilingual education is the most effective model to promote additive bilingualism (Thomas and Collier, 2002) he recognises that this option is not likely to be available to most bilingual children. It is certainly not practical in the many schools in Britain in which a wide range of languages is spoken.

Cummins suggests that in the absence of actual bilingual education, incorporating the language and culture of pupils and involving families and the community in the education of their children can empower students from minority communities to achieve in mainstream education (1986; 2000). The concept of Identity Texts (children being supported to explore personal experience and identity in their different languages) was developed to enable pupils to build on prior knowledge and take greater control of their own learning in mainstream classrooms in situations where the power differential between cultures is substantial (Cummins *et al*, 2006).

The history of the development of dual language books shows teachers working very much along these principles as they build partnerships with parents and draw on their expertise to bring the language and culture of the home into the school, encourage children's creativity and participation in their own learning, and recognise skills in home languages often ignored in mainstream education.

Developments in the study of multiliteracy have led to the exploration of literacy practices in families and communities that use several languages in the course of their day to day life.

The Multiliteracy debate

The Linguistic Minorities Report carried out a major investigation into the prevalence and usage of the languages of new minorities in England with detailed surveys carried out in Coventry, Bradford and Haringey (LMP, 1985). Although the work of the LMP was never followed up, the study raised awareness of language use and literacy development in new communities. In particular it brought to the attention of educationists the existence of mother tongue schools that taught the languages of the community. The debate around the importance of teaching first languages was reflected in the Swann Report (DES, 1985), which recommended that the teaching of community languages remain the responsibility of individual communities, thereby denying communities the opportunity of having their languages taught in mainstream schools.

Teachers and researchers throughout the 1990s began to take a new interest in the role of community languages, their importance in defining personal identity and the uses made of literacy in different communities and social contexts. The New Literacy Studies provided a theoretical framework for the developing research into multiliteracy. The work of Street (1984, 2000) challenged the concept of 'autonomous literacy' as a universally applicable concept. Researchers began to focus on literacy events and literacy practices used for specific purposes and grounded in social and cultural practices in specific communities and contexts (Street, 1993; Barton, 1991). The developing interest in literacy practices in multilingual settings began to

> focus attention on the multiple ways people draw on to combine the codes in their communicative repertoires to make meaning as they negotiate and display cultural identities and social relationships. (Hornberger, 2000:357).

Barton has commented on the little recognition given to the literacy traditions in British Asian homes (1994) and Gregory has noted the absence of mainstream research into the experience of new language learners (2008b: 14). It is interesting that many researchers who explored the concept of multi-literacies started their careers as teachers who came into contact with the hidden language and literacy skills and practices of the children in their classrooms. It was in the children's homes and in their communities that these skills were revealed and it is there that the researchers went to find out about children's 'unofficial literacies' (Gregory and Williams, 2000).

Children of Bangladeshi heritage in east London who spoke Sylheti in the home were studied in a range of out-of-school literacy activities, learning standard Bengali in community classes and studying the Qur'an in Arabic at madressas (Islamic schools), both activities crucial to their identities as British Bangladeshi Muslims. The children were observed engaging with the literacy practices of the home, using their different skills for different purposes to '... mix and blend practices from home and school to unique new patterns and forms' (Gregory and Williams, 2000:52). Studies revealed the important role of family members such as siblings (Rashid and Gregory, 1997) and grandparents as mediators of literacy as well as the creative two-way process of intergenerational learning in a range of languages and media (Kenner et al, 2004).

The concept of syncretic literacy was developed to describe the experiences of the children and the ways in which they come to learn different forms of literacy associated with different methodologies and different cultural values, and to take account of the social context of learning. The process of simultaneous learning shows children as highly active learners creating new forms out of the different literacies that co-exist in their lives, understanding their different purposes and associating them with their own developing identities (Gregory, Long and Volk, 2004).

Kenner's work with 3 and 4 year old children in nursery classes (2000a) has been influential in helping monolingual teachers to understand how, far from being confused by different languages and scripts, young children benefit greatly when the literacy practices of the home are incorporated into school and are found 'actively re-interpreting texts and practices for their own purposes' (Kenner, 2000b:127)

Kenner's study of children aged 6 becoming biliterate in Chinese, Arabic and Spanish focuses on the simultaneous aspects of bilingual learning as the children are observed learning to write at home, in their community school and in their primary school. In different learning contexts, with different teaching methods and materials, the children explore the ways in which their languages and writing systems work and reveal their understanding in the process of teaching each other. Kenner concludes that 'The different experiences gained in each setting complement each other, giving greater access to knowledge' (Kenner, 2004:152). On this issue Edwards explains how experiencing different languages through different pedagogical styles enables children to see 'literacies as systems' (Edwards, 2009:90).

In her studies of young bilingual children becoming literate, Datta explores children's home literacy experiences with a particular focus on the cultural and linguistic knowledge that they bring to bear on their learning of English. She draws attention to the increasing availability of a range of visual media in community languages. How this impacts on children's reading comprehension is demonstrated in her example of children's understanding of metaphor in Bollywood songs (Datta, 2007:32).

There is little opportunity for children in mainstream schools to have access to bilingual education. Many children attend complementary classes organised by their communities to learn the language of the family. Opportunities to study community languages have recently increased as some secondary schools offer them as modern languages at exam level (Ofsted, 2008) and some primary schools have taken up the option of teaching them. The study of language use and pedagogical practices in complementary schools is very recent. A major ethnographic study of Gujarati schools in Leicester (Martin et al, 2006) reveals how both Gujarati and English are used simultaneously to support learning.

The high concentration of Bengali speaking bilinguals in Tower Hamlets has offered opportunities to explore the possibilities offered by simultaneous learning in Bengali and English in both mainstream and complementary schools. Kenner et al have worked with second and third generation children to explore the benefits to children who have become dominant in English of using both their languages to gain a deeper understanding of, for example, a traditional Bengali poem (2008c) or to carry out a mathematical investigation (2008b). Current research continues to explore the possibilities offered by partnership teaching between teachers in mainstream and complementary schools.

With respect to the specific use of dual language books, although they have been in use for many years in classrooms, there has been very little work since Ming Tsow's 1986 study to show how children use their language skills to read the two languages on the page. The present study was designed to explore how this particular learning resource contributes to simultaneous literacy learning. It was informed by three pieces of recent research which built on the use of dual language books. A dozen third generation Londoners aged 11, who used a dialect of Gujarati in their everyday lives in the home, retold *The Raja's Big Ears* (Desai, 1989) in Gujarati, a story that they had encountered in a dual language version. The study shows how they came to terms with the unfamiliar standard Gujarati of the story and how they reinterpreted it in their own way:

> reflecting the oral tradition of the home rather than the book tradition of the school. In so doing they demonstrated their skill at adapting their language to the discourse conventions appropriate in the different social contexts of their everyday lives. (Sneddon and Patel, 2003:383)

Robertson studied third generation children of Pakistani descent learning simultaneously in two languages using different scripts. The children in their Urdu class used a dual language version of *Lima's Red Hot Chilli* (Mills, 2000). Robertson notes how the teacher capitalised on the children's knowledge of both languages in the book, also using Pahari and making reference to their knowledge of Arabic from Qur'anic classes to explore and compare the texts at all language levels, making full use of the children's high level of meta-linguistic awareness (Robertson, 2006:179; Gregory *et al*, 2004)

As an introduction to an exploration of children learning to read in a new language in a variety of contexts, Gregory introduces Annie, aged 7, who can read in Thai and is learning English using a traditional Thai fable in a dual language book. The close observation and analysis of the strategies used by Annie draws attention to the challenges presented by a dual language book when the child has an unequal understanding of both languages. Her lesser knowledge of English means that Annie does not have access to prediction as a reading strategy, thereby making the English translation far more challenging to read than the original Thai text. On the other hand, the dual language format strongly supports the development of new vocabulary.

The last two studies in particular demonstrate how, with major differences in script, grammar and orthographic principles between their languages, the children bring into play a wide range of creative strategies that demonstrate their extensive cultural, linguistic and metalinguistic knowledge and understanding.

All these studies provide examples of children learning different languages in different settings with different teaching methods and achieving a personal synthesis that deepens their understanding of how language works. As children compare and contrast their learning experiences, play school, teach each other, learn from family members, explore language structure and blend and create new strategies, they are actively shaping their identities as learners. The recent research into multiliteracies and the development of the concept of syncretic literacy has highlighted the essential role of family and community members acting as mediators of literacy (Gregory *et al*, 2004).

The role of families and communities

Throughout the 1980s and 1990s there was a wealth of literature on the subject of parents' involvement in reading with their children at home in English. The Haringey Project had a considerable impact on educational thinking as it provided evidence that children's reading scores could be improved by the simple process of reading with their parents on a regular basis and that this benefit applied to children across the full ability range. With respect to bilingual children, the study reported that:

> some children read to parents who could not themselves read English, or, in a few cases cannot read at all. (Tizard, Schofield and Hewison, 1982:14)

The Haringey study was influential in promoting home school reading schemes and further research. The PACT (Parents and Children and Teachers) scheme in Hackney developed from it and was proactive in encouraging the involvement of bilingual parents (PACT, 1984:39). PACT was responsible for the production of the dual language books in Kurdish described in Chapter 1.

While the movement initiated by the Haringey study was broadly successful in raising children's reading attainment, it operated a one-way system by which the school advised parents on how they should support their children. This process has been criticised for bringing the powerful (and essentially monolingual) model of learning promoted by the school into the home with the potential to devalue the family's existing literacy practices. As Gregory and Williams have noted (2000), it is rare for schools to enquire into the literacy practices of the home and researchers have expressed concern about the lack of knowledge and awareness that schools have about the literacy experiences of bilingual children (Martin-Jones and Jones, 2000:10).

The models that have been found to be successful in empowering pupils from minority communities have stressed the importance of a two-way process of collaboration with families, of a genuine partnership between families, communities and schools that operates at different levels of the education system (Faltis, 1995) and directly engages community organisations in the work of the school (Sneddon, 1997). The concept of Funds of Knowledge developed by Moll in Arizona (Gonzalez *et al*, 1993) encouraged teachers to enquire into the skills and knowledge of families and build these into their curriculum and classroom practice.

All the studies of literacy practices in multilingual communities mentioned here have engaged closely with families and communities: observing literacy practices in a range of social, cultural and linguistic contexts, engaging with parents, siblings and grandparents and revealing their crucial role as mediators of literacy (Gregory and Biarnès, 1994; Gregory *et al*, 1993; Williams, 1997; Kenner *et al*, 2004). The more recent studies of practices in complementary school settings (Conteh, 2007; Martin *et al*, 2006; Robertson, 2006) have begun to document language use, pedagogical practices, teaching materials used and the impact of these on children's achievement and personal and learner identities. In the absence of bilingual education in mainstream schools, exploring how bilingual children negotiate meaning between their two languages necessarily involves working closely with their families to find out how they use their languages at home and in the community, thereby revealing the hidden literacies of the home.

The teachers who developed the dual language books discussed in Chapter 1 all engaged closely with the language and cultural knowledge of parents and communities: as a source of original stories, as story tellers in the classroom, as translators of text, voices on tape, advisers on illustrations and public performances. Those who, like Clover and Gilbert, organised dual language book-making workshops, made full use of families' cultural and linguistic Funds of Knowledge to make books of high personal significance to their children. As they reported, the partnerships built through this process often led to a greater confidence (and sometimes improved knowledge of English) in parents and to their much closer engagement with their children's schooling.

The benefits of this process were discovered by the Basic Skills Unit in 1993 when it developed the concept of Family Literacy with the brief to break the 'recurring intergeneration cycle of low attainment' (Brooks *et al*,1996:1) by working with children and parents together.

The parents studied by the researchers above had, in most cases, access to community classes for their children and/or some resources in the family language with which to teach their children. Kenner mentions magazines, calendars, children's primers, books of rhymes and, of course, books sent home by community classes. She has demonstrated the benefits of incorporating these genuine home literacy materials into the school classroom (Kenner, 2000a). Many parents have difficulty in obtaining materials for children in the language of the home, however. The issue is often one of demography: where communities and social networks are denser, complementary classes and resources such as books and magazines are more likely to be available.

The children who feature in the present study had no ready access to complementary classes and all of their parents referred to the difficulty of obtaining books and teaching materials for children. The supply of dual language books provided by the teachers had offered the first opportunity they had had to read in the language of the home with their children. The books were greatly welcomed in spite of the limitations of their cultural content. The mothers of Magda and Albana had only one book each in Albanian, neither of them accessible to young children. The dual language books and the encouragement they received from the teachers enabled them to develop their children's biliteracy, to improve their own English skills, to become more involved in their children's learning and, in both cases, provided stepping stones towards professional training in education. Through their growing reading and writing skills, their daughters found new ways of exploring their evolving identities as British Albanians and as learners.

3

Issues in identity

Teachers who have used the language and culture of the home as a resource know well the children's joy and pride at having their personal experience affirmed. They report the increase in children's motivation and the beneficial effect on their learning and achievement. In the interactions between children and their teachers, identities are negotiated, for better or worse. Cummins explains how

> when students' developing sense of self is affirmed and extended through their interactions with teachers, they are more likely to apply themselves to academic effort and participate actively in their instruction. (Cummins, 1996:2)

The use of dual language books can support the negotiation of personal identity and highlight aspects of learner identity as children learn to read in their home language. The present chapter considers recent research on identity that is relevant to children in multilingual classrooms and, in particular, to the children who feature in the present study.

New identities – new ethnicities

Identities are about how we live our everyday lives. As families migrate around the world and create new diasporas, new communities settle and personal identities and commitments cut across geographical boundaries. Individuals bring with them the traditions and languages of the country of origin and find themselves living with new ones. As globalisation and humanitarian crises increase population mobility, trajectories of migration become increasingly complex. As well as living in two or more languages, individuals may experience many different cultures on their journey. These cultures impact in different ways on different aspects of everyday life at different times. 'Cultures of hybridity' develop as individuals negotiate their way

43

between different aspects of their lives (Hall, 1992). In the same way that patterns of language use vary from individual to individual, so does the way in which they engage with and define themselves with respect to the cultures in their environment.

The model of identity developed by Pavlenko and Blackledge (2004) acknowledges the significant power differentials between the standard and minority languages in societies that are officially monolingual. Multidimensional identities take account of age, gender, class, ethnicity and sexual orientation. Some of these aspects are fixed but others, such as language, are more flexible and change and evolve according to time, place and circumstance. Identities can be voluntarily assumed; they can be externally imposed by a dominant language and culture; imposed identities can be challenged, resisted and negotiated. New identities can be consciously created imaginatively through symbolic links as communities and individuals seek meaning and coherence in their personal narratives. These aspects of identity are relevant to the bilingual pupils in British schools as they experience social and educational environments that reproduce social inequalities and can deny or limit identity options.

Language and identity: debates and stereotypes

The position of minority ethnic communities in relation to national identity features regularly in political discourse and in the press. While some recent educational policy highlights the benefits of bilingualism to the individual and to society (DfES 2003, CILT, 2008), public debate regularly undermines this pluralist vision and affirms a common sense model that associates monolingualism with social harmony. For example, a politician responding to youth riots in the north of England used a discourse that linked multilingualism with 'lack of English' and non-English speaking mothers with violence and social disorder (Blackledge, 2004). Public discourse of this nature devalues children's personal experience.

Schools may be keen to develop a multicultural curriculum but, in the absence of a detailed knowledge of their local community, there can be many pitfalls. Newly qualified teachers have received little training to teach children from diverse communities and report a lack of confidence. As a result, assumptions are made about community practices based on limited knowledge and stereotypes are rife. Harris raises this issue and expresses concern with the fossilisation of culture implied in the concept of 'ethnic absolutism' which

... encapsulates the experience of seeing the rich variety of dispositions and behaviours of individuals and groups in family and community settings reduced to crude, supposedly eternal, essences. (2006: 6)

Naïve views of such issues in education fail to recognise the flexible and fluid nature of boundaries between culture and language use and reduce the multicultural curriculum to tokenistic and fossilised 'saris, steel bands and samosas' (Troyna and Williams, 1986).

The multicultural curriculum can end up reinforcing stereotypes, sitting uncomfortably as an add-on to the National Curriculum; it then fails to address the needs of the children or to acknowledge or build on their knowledge and experience. There is a lot for teachers to learn about culture and language and many rewards for both pupils and teachers from learning it, but there are pitfalls on the way. Current policies that recommend that schools get to know and reach out to their communities and build partnerships with parents may help the process (DCSF, 2007).

Harris has a parallel concern about what he calls 'romantic bilingualism'. Most schools keep records of the languages spoken in pupils' homes but these are often recorded without thorough enquiry. A lack of knowledge about multilingual societies, educational opportunities and family trajectories can lead teachers to make faulty assumptions about language and literacy practices and competences in the home (Harris, 1997). In such circumstances it happens that teachers send home letters translated into a language that no one in the family can read.

This issue is particularly relevant for teachers who wish to support pupils' use of community languages through using dual language books. Unless teachers have some knowledge of whether pupils, or their families, can understand, speak, read or write in a particular language, sending the books home may be inappropriate. The books can only be deployed effectively in the context of a school that has good relationships with parents and knowledge of families' literacy practices. The latter point was important to the success of the present study: the teachers started from a sound knowledge of the languages in everyday use in the children's homes and had established that parents were both willing and able to read with their children in those languages.

The role of language is crucial in the development of personal identity. In the context of a study of young British students of South Asian heritage, Harris has shown what an exploration of the pattern of everyday language use can reveal about their cultural allegiance and their personal identities. In particular he has noted the many cases in which students refer to 'my language' and 'my religion' and claim allegiance to a language and to a religion that may be imperfectly known and little practised (Harris, 2006).

A study of complementary schools in Leicester that teach Gujarati has documented the important role that the schools play by providing safe spaces in which pupils can explore and develop their personal identities (Creese *et al*, 2006). For the majority of bilingual children, complementary schools are the only sites where they can learn the language and literacy of their communities. The schools, developed by the communities themselves, receive little official recognition or funding. The children who attend them belong to the third generation of the community and are generally more confident speakers of English than of Gujarati. Although children in the present study are learning the language of their community in very different circumstances, there are similarities in the way the opportunities offered to them provide a space in which they can develop personal identities.

Creese *et al* suggest that the Leicester schools enable the exploration of three aspects of personal identities that are '... dynamic and multiple rather than unitary and fixed' (Creese *et al*, 2006:25). Although they are now dominant in English, for the pupils who attend the schools and their families, the maintenance of the Gujarati language is a crucial part of their heritage and is essential to enable communication with all generations in the Leicester community and beyond, in the countries from which their families have originated. Within a monolingual educational environment, the schools provide a safe space in which the pupils' heritage culture and language are valued and promoted. The pupils study Gujarati, learn about literature and aspects of Gujarati culture and have a range of language options to communicate with their teachers and peers.

Complementary schools offer opportunities for pupils to explore aspects of their identity as 'successful student learners' (p34) that are different from those available in their mainstream schools. The pupils learn bilingually, using all their language resources in a different pedagogical environment. They have the opportunity to succeed in a subject not available in the mainstream school. Pupils in complementary schools are commonly entered for GCSE and A level exams at an early age and obtain high grades. This has a significant effect on their confidence as learners.

Creese *et al* also note the opportunities offered by complementary schools to develop multicultural identities that are very different from the stereotypical ones that may be on offer in the mainstream school. The pupils' ability to move between languages and cultures in fluid, flexible ways can lead to greater linguistic and cultural sophistication.

Dual language books and personal identity

In Ma's study, referred to in Chapter 2, the Chinese mother teaches her child to read using a dual language book, *Lima's Red Hot Chilli* (Mills, 2000) which has a South Asian British context. Although she did not have a book with a Chinese connection, the mother is still shown 'connecting the meaning conveyed by the text with the meaning in the home culture', creating a bridge between the culture of the book and the culture of the home. An example is the way in which she uses the Chinese metaphor of 'burning eyebrows' to help Minnie understand the response of a character in the story (Ma, 2008:244).

There are many accounts from teachers of the delight expressed by children who first encounter a book in their classroom in the language that is spoken in their home. A good example of this in the case studies is the pleasure that Magda and Albana derived from being offered a selection of stories in Albanian and English. Their mothers were delighted to find this resource and the girls rapidly worked their way through all available texts. Similarly it was an encounter with favourite English stories in Turkish and English that got Lek and Durkan excited and motivated them to work together to read in Turkish.

Learning about children's lives and using this knowledge to build the curriculum and affirm children's identities was at the heart of most of the dual language book projects reported in the first chapter of this book. As well as valuing children's home languages and using them to make stories accessible to children, the Newham project, the Reading Materials for Minority Groups Project and the Kurdish book project were about introducing children's cultures into the school. They sought traditional stories from families and made them widely available as printed books to all children. The same motivation applied to the books more recently developed in Somali (John), Nepali (Baker) and Gujarati (Ashraf). An example from the case studies was Mydda's encounter with *The Moving Mango Tree* collection of stories in Urdu and English (Jabeen, 1992) and her pleasure in discovering that one of the stories, The Bad Crow, was a favourite bedtime one told to her by her mother.

However, it is the dual language books made in writing workshops, for and with individual children, based on their personal experience, that make the greatest impact on children. The content of the work, generally negotiated between a child and parent or teacher, reflects the interests and language use of a child at a particular point in their life. Clover and Gilbert's small child, who carried her special book in her teeth, demonstrated the importance to individual children of the special books made with them. Other teachers have had the experience of meeting children as long as twenty years after the event and being told how the special book has been treasured over the years.

After the end of the observations reported in Chapter 5, Magda and Albana made personal books with their mothers about their experiences on holiday in Albania. Not only did they display and read them to all their friends in school, but Magda took hers with her when she attended her very first Albanian lesson at a complementary school. The children in her class were so impressed that their Albanian teacher decided that she would take on the making of dual language books as a class project for all children to encourage the development of their writing.

Personal books and identity texts

The connection between book making and identity is made explicit in the Canadian project described below. Dual language books have developed in the US and in Canada since the 1980s, in much the same way as they have in the UK. In the US, they were originally focused on the needs of Latino children and published in Spanish and English. More recently, publishers have produced books in the languages and cultures of other large bilingual populations, such as Chinese, Korean, Vietnamese and Urdu (Ernst-Slavit and Mulhern, 2006). Among the advantages noted in the Canadian context was the way in which the books can support a teacher to engage with children's languages in a class in which many different ones are spoken.

Identity Texts are personal texts written by children, with the help of adults where necessary, in classroom based writing workshops. They aim to promote bilingual writing in the classroom as a means of acknowledging a child's experience. The practice and research in Canada have shown this process to be particularly supportive of children who have recently arrived in a new country and are coming to terms with a new language and a new culture (Cummins *et al*, 2006).

Newcomers are offered the opportunity to make full use of their existing language skills and the prior knowledge and experience that has shaped their identities and their cognitive functioning. As well as providing a space that enables children to express their feelings as they come to terms with new experiences, the strategy makes full use of the transfer of knowledge and skills between languages, acts as a scaffold for their writing and can change their perceptions of themselves and the image others have of them. As one student expresses it:

> When I am allowed to use Urdu in class it helps me because when I write in Urdu and then I look at Urdu words and English comes in my mind. So, it help me a lot. When I write in English, Urdu comes in my mind. When I read in English I say it in Urdu in my mind. When I read in Urdu I feel very comfortable because I can understand it. (Cummins *et al*, 2006:8)

Through developing a pedagogy of respect for the knowledge and experience of students, teachers create a classroom ethos that encourages students to negotiate and invest their developing identities and to gain confidence and take control of their own learning.

Identity texts can be developed through a range of modern media which can make children's work accessible to a world-wide audience. As well as producing dual language texts in print form for use by peers in school, the websites of Thornwood and Peel Schools, involved in the Canadian research, provide a showcase for examples of writing in many different formats and languages.

A Friend (1995)

The text reveals the importance to a child, disoriented by his experiences in an unfamiliar language and culture, of a chance meeting with someone who spoke his language and became his friend. Luisa Pieris, a teacher in his Hackney Primary school, encouraged him to work with his mother to tell his story, in the context of the bilingual mother and child writing group described in Chapter 1.

The boy listened to us because we were speaking Arabic. He came and asked me in Arabic: 'where are you from?' I said: 'I come from Iraq and I am Muslim.' The boy said: 'I come from Yemen and I am Jewish'. I said:'shall we be friends?' The boy said yes.

Mohamed, a Muslim child recently arrived from Iraq as a refugee, tells the story of how a Jewish child from the Yemen, living on the same housing estate, overheard him speaking Arabic to his mother and how they became friends on the basis of a shared language. When Mohamed's family were re-housed he was sad to lose contact with his friend. One day, by accident, on his way to his new school, he met his old friend in the street and discovered that they now went to neighbouring schools: Mohamed to a mainstream primary, his friend to a Jewish school. The two schools had been developing a partnership, with children visiting each other for special assemblies. Mohamed was very proud to read his story to an assembly that included children from his friend's school.

Multiple identities and learning from dual language books in the case studies

As the children in the present study learned to read with dual language books, their conversations revealed responses to texts, changes in attitudes and interests and connections made with different aspects of their environment that provide clues to their developing identities. The following explores some of the issues that arose in the case studies in the light of the work of Creese *et al* in complementary schools.

Heritage identities

The use of dual language books in the classroom can indicate a positive approach to language diversity. It can, as mentioned by Cummins, create confidence and pride and enable children to explore their cultures simultaneously rather than keeping them in completely separate domains. Imaginative responses to texts can create new identity options.

The two Turkish speaking children who feature in Chapter 7, **Lek** and **Durkan**, first encountered the dual language books in a group session designed to improve their English. They were delighted and begged their teacher to let them try to read them in Turkish. The stories available to them were all translations of traditional European folk tales which they knew well in English and there was nothing at all about Turkey in the books. However the recordings show evidence of the children living in simultaneous worlds: speaking like the London-born children in their school but spontaneously connecting their reading to personal experiences, linking the turnip in *The Giant Turnip* to the pickled turnip drink sold in local Turkish shops, talking about the books and play station games that they have in Turkish at home, advising the researcher on the best way to learn Turkish and bursting into a competitive performance of Turkish hand clapping rhymes.

Magda and **Albana** had been very isolated from the Albanian community at the point when they became involved in the study. The use of dual language books was standard practice in their classroom and, with the support of their mothers, they jumped at the opportunity to learn to read Albanian. They had no books in Albanian at home and none of the many dual language books they borrowed from school reflected Albanian culture. As the school valued their developing biliteracy and invited them to read in assembly, their confidence and pride grew and both of them, especially Albana, started using Albanian much more in the home. When an Albanian lunchtime club was set up they welcomed the opportunities it offered to perform dance and poetry in public. Chapter 5 follows them as they develop from emergent biliterates to performers and authors of their own dual language books.

The identity issue was more complex for **Sarah**, as indeed it is for the many children who originate from countries where the language of education is different from the regional languages and dialects spoken by most of the population. As a quiet and reserved child, working on her own, she had little opportunity to share her learning with a group. As a result of the colonial legacy, French is the language of public communication and education in the Democratic Republic of Congo. It is the language her parents chose to use primarily with her. They also used Lingala among themselves but, although Sarah could understand the gist of their private conversations, she could not speak the language. Being biliterate in French was a great source of pride, but the literature she read bore little connection with her family's country of origin. She was delighted when the researcher gave her a dual language book in Lingala and French, bought for her in Paris, even though, as a short illustrated folk tale, it was designed for much younger children.

For **Mydda**, learning to read in Urdu with her mother reconnected her with her Urdu heritage and the language she spoke with limited fluency. After a summer visit from her grandmother and cousins from Pakistan, she enjoyed using an Urdu primer and asking her mother about unfamiliar pictures, like that of the 'pudding man'. Mydda's mother took every opportunity to discuss issues of culture and language that arose from both the dual language books and the resources from Pakistan. Mydda loved *The Bad Crow*, a favourite story that her mother used to tell her in Urdu. But even the Urdu text of the culturally African story of *Handa's Surprise* (Browne, 1994) provoked a lengthy conversation about the varieties of orange you can get in Pakistan that are not available in England. Mydda loved the children's poems and rhymes introduced by her mother, she knew many of them by heart and spontaneously performed them for the researcher.

Learner identities

As Creese *et al* found, the children's learner identities developed. The study enabled all of them, in different ways, to see themselves and to be seen in a new light as a result of exploring or expanding a new area of learning. It was most dramatic in the case of **Mydda**, the competent reader who had a ten minute attention span and didn't enjoy reading. As she approached the complexities of de-coding Urdu script as a puzzle to be solved, she became curious, persistent and very determined to make sense of the texts in front of her. The ten minute attention span became an hour and the effect of her commitment translated back into a greater interest in reading in English.

Neither **Lek** nor **Durkan** were good readers in any language. However, the opportunity to work together to read simultaneously in both languages helped them to discover a range of strategies they could deploy between them to decode and understand text and they found the process very enjoyable. Their reading attention span increased considerably and, like Mydda, they were keen to extend the observation sessions.

The main discovery for **Sarah** was that she could read and enjoy much more sophisticated literary texts than had previously been available to her in French and that, as she began to explore the new skill of writing in French, she was well on her way to becoming a very competent biliterate.

Magda and **Albana** made a similar journey to Sarah's with respect to writing. They had enjoyed learning to read in English and the skills and determination they deployed to read in Albanian led them, like Mydda, to become better readers in English too. The very public acknowledgement of their developing skills was a great source of pride and they enjoyed their identity as biliterates, using their knowledge to lead and support less experienced children in the Albanian club that was started at their school.

Mohamed's learner identity was invested in being very articulate and literate in English for his age. As a moderately fluent speaker of Gujarati in domestic settings, the encounter with the written form in a very different script presented a challenge which he was beginning to address with increasing determination as the formal observation period came to an end.

The multicultural dimension
The dual language books encountered in the classroom can affirm children's linguistic identity; if their content reflects the culture of the child's home, they will affirm that also. A number of classrooms display posters and teaching resources that reflect the children's heritage. But the visual environment is not enough in itself. Ultimately it is how these resources are put to use in the everyday work of the class that will determine whether a genuine intercultural understanding is promoted in the classroom. Kenner has long advocated the display and use in the classroom of authentic resources that reflect the literacy practices of children's homes (Kenner, 2000a). Gravelle has

written of the value of having children's books published in a range of languages and imported from the countries of origin in school and class libraries (1996). Such resources are particularly valuable for the more advanced reader, for whom little is available in dual language format. Sarah in the present study was frustrated by this lack, and would have greatly benefited from finding original children's literature in French in the library. The selection and use of such materials is a good opportunity to engage the community and to obtain support for children from parents as well as from the school staff's own language resources.

The most readily available dual language books, and the ones mostly used in the present study, are published commercially, the same story being produced in up to 30 languages. While most will inevitably fail to match the cultural background of the children, these books have a particular value. As used by Magda and Albana's teacher, they enabled her to teach reading in English and to send them home to be read in the home language with the families. The teacher could then discuss the children's progress and understanding of the book across languages in class, as they had all read the same story. Alongside other multilingual materials there are many ways in which the books can be used to compare and contrast linguistic features and to develop all children's interest in languages. Many suggestions for activities of this nature are found in the work of Kenner (2004), Gregory (2008b), Conteh (2003) and Datta and Pomphrey (2004).

Children's enjoyment of stories from a range of cultures was much in evidence in the present study. They knew how to connect, for example, the African fruit from *Handa's Surprise* with the many oranges in Pakistan, the enormous turnip of the traditional European story with the pickled turnip drink, bringing together elements of the children's present day life in Britain with elements from different and more personal experiences.

The best way for teachers to avoid creating stereotypes when introducing unfamiliar cultures to the classroom is to build directly on the experience of the children and their families. It is in the writing of bilingual texts from personal experience that young children will explore the authentic reality of their personal identities and, where offered an opportunity to celebrate and share them, will foster genuine multicultural understanding and a culture of respect.

4
Issues in translation

The opening chapter described how bilingual parents, teachers and teaching assistants translated texts for use in school and how special projects and, later, commercial publishers, gradually built up the bank of texts and the range of languages. As more books became available, all kinds of questions arose about the purpose, quality and educational value of the books. Those who have never translated are rarely aware of the many layers of complexity and difficulty involved and commonly assume that it is sufficient to know the two languages concerned.

Dual language books are a valuable classroom resource for supporting language learning, exploring languages, affirming identity. But their use in the classroom is not unproblematic and they may not always be the best resource for bilingual pupils. This chapter explores some of the issues involved in translating texts for dual language books, such as the status, purpose and function of texts and the cultural and linguistic choices that need to be made, building on existing research on the translation of children's literature.

Translation studies is a discipline within the field of applied linguistics. The translation of children's literature has until recently been a much neglected area of study (Lathey, 2006). While texts for children referred to in recent translation studies are published as free-standing texts in independent volumes, much of the research describes issues and processes which apply in varying degrees to the production of dual language texts. Some of the key principles and parameters explored by researchers in the translation of children's literature are described below and discussed with particular reference to dual language books.

The status, purpose and function of children's literature in translation
Status of texts

Children's literature is usually produced by adults for children: writers, illustrators, publishers and editors provide the books; teachers and librarians make them available; parents buy a lot of them, especially those aimed at younger children. In the English speaking world the term children's literature covers the whole range from board books for babies to 'cross-over' books for older teenagers and adults. Because books for younger children are often read aloud by adults, they can include whole layers of meaning expressed through metaphor, word play and irony aimed at the adult reader (O'Connell, 1999).

The canon of high quality literature for children is not easy to define. Texts vary greatly in quality and value and there are many different genres and traditions. Texts originally written for adults, such as *Robinson Crusoe* or *Gulliver's Travels*, have been endlessly abridged, modified, bowdlerised, re-written, translated and re-translated to meet the criteria of what is deemed suitable for children at different times and in different places. The tales of the Brothers Grimm, the adventure novels of Jules Verne and *Alice in Wonderland*, among many others, are known as children's classics the world over, but it is quite a shock for older readers when they encounter the original versions and find how different they are from the tales they read and loved as children (Shavit, 1986).

An additional layer of alteration intervenes when such texts are translated. There are well over 30 translations and adaptations of *Alice in Wonderland* into German: from simplified versions (missing out the nonsense, the irony, the complex language and the metaphors) to close translations of the integral text supported by pages of scholarly footnotes aimed at the adult reader. O'Sullivan considers that none of these has ever captured the spirit and the originality of Carroll's text (2001).

The purpose and function of children's literature

So why are children's texts so readily and frequently modified? Historically, texts for children have served a didactic and socialising function or been used directly in religious and moral instruction. Their role as entertainment is more recent. The moral and social values which influence the upbringing of children vary from society to society and change over time. Writers have great faith in their power to influence children's behaviour so fairy tales, fables and classical texts get rewritten to provide messages and models of behaviour that are approved in any given society at a particular time (Fernandez Lopez,

2000). The didactic role of children's literature is very much in evidence in the books we choose for the classroom.

Social attitudes in Britain have changed. Creating a successful multicultural society means challenging racist and xenophobic attitudes. Material that reflects such attitudes is not considered acceptable in modern English language children's literature. Changes have been introduced into classic texts such as Enid Blyton's and Roald Dahl's. More recent children's books are careful, not only to avoid derogatory comments, but to promote positive images of people from different ethnic backgrounds and with different abilities. Traditional stories with male leading characters have been rewritten with female ones: several authors have written versions of *Jill and the Beanstalk* (Gregory, 2004; Vega, 1997; Walker, 1996).

The purpose and function of dual language books
Helping to understand English
When teachers encounter children who are new to English, their first priority is generally to ensure that they have some understanding of the classroom curriculum to enable them to follow lessons. Chapter 1 outlined how teachers initially produced their own resources with amateur translators. Commercial publishers did not always improve quality:

> The insensitivity of publishers to the complexities of multilingual resources has often resulted in inadequate translations which greatly diminish the usefulness of dual language books. (Edwards and Walker, 1996)

As specialised publishers became involved, standards rose, but the translation of children's literature remains a difficult area given the great shortage of translators experienced in both children's literature and community languages. Providing access to an English text remains one of the most popular functions of dual language books; this function is well supported by audio media such as tapes, CDs and innovations like the Talking Pen.

Reflecting culture, language and identity
It is an exciting experience for a recently arrived child to find in her classroom a text, from her family's country of origin, that tells a familiar tale or illustrates aspects of life in that country. For many children this has provided a starting point to talk about personal experience, to share knowledge and to take pride in their cultural identity. Reflecting culture was one of the main aims of the specially funded projects that developed dual language books. Roger Hancock, who produced the Kurdish/English books described in Chapter 1, explains their purpose:

It was felt that the publication of Kurdish folktales would serve to welcome newly arrived children and parents, give formal recognition to their literacy and culture and provide support for the learning of English as a second language. (1993:1)

The Refugee Council published collections of stories to reinforce the cultural identity of children in the vulnerable position of asylum seekers and refugees.

Reflecting culture as well as language is a common aim across a number of specially funded and commercially produced dual language book projects in Britain and other countries. For example, the French publisher L'Harmattan has an extensive catalogue of traditional stories and modern life-style tales from countries in Africa and Asia; the American publisher East West Discovery Press groups its extensive list according to the culture the books represent.

Widening cultural experience through sharing stories
Meek notes the value of stories in translation from other languages to widen children's experience, introduce them to classic texts from children's literature and 'interpret other cultures' (Meek, 2001:xiii). In the English speaking world, we have come to take for granted the great variety and quality of texts available for children of all ages, due to the size of the market. As a result of this abundance, there is a great deal of translation of children's literature from English into other languages, but much less from other languages into English (Fernandez Lopez, 2000).

Language choices in the translation of children's literature
The relationship between source text and target language
Anyone who has been asked to translate a lengthy communication from a headteacher to parents will be familiar with the great debate in translation: will the translated letter remain close to its source text or will it get reinterpreted to fit more closely to the target language and culture? Translators are faced with many linguistic and cultural decisions and most translated texts end up somewhere along a continuum between the fairly literal translation and a reinterpretation.

Translators of children's literature and the theoretical models with which they engage position themselves differently in relation to this continuum and focus on different aspects of it. For example Toury's model refers to 'adequacy' to describe a translation that is faithful to the source text. 'Acceptability' describes one that is closer to the literary norms of the target language (Puurtinen, 1994).

Shavit suggests that

> The final product of the act of translation is the result of the relationship be-
> tween a source system and a target system, a relationship that is itself deter-
> mined by a certain hierarchy of semiotic constraints. (Shavit, 1986:25)

Her model introduces two complementary principles that govern the translation of texts for children and which are of particular relevance to the translation of dual language books.

The first, 'translators adjust the text for what is considered 'good for the child"
refers to the didactic function of children's literature. Translators working to
this principle need to be aware of the norms prevalent in the target culture.

The second, 'translators adjust the text to a child's ability to read and comprehend' takes into account both the linguistic constraints, such as vocabulary
and sentence structure, and the level of 'foreignness' which children may be
deemed to understand. This principle requires translators to have a fairly
precise idea of the target audience for the text: the age of the children, for
example, and their expected levels of literacy.

These principles, taken together, locate Shavit's model at the 'acceptability'
end of Toury's continuum and can lead to major alterations and adaptations
to a text. At the extreme end of the 'acceptability' continuum, a new text can
be developed which is far removed from the source and so well adapted to the
target language and culture that it is not readily identified as a translation at
all. Fables and fairy tales from Aesop, the Panchatantra, the brothers Grimm,
Perrault and La Fontaine, for example, appear in endless variations over
space and time so that many readers are surprised when they discover a
version of the same story from a different culture and are equally surprised to
find that what they thought was a traditional English tale has its origins else-
where.

An interesting challenge is presented by texts whose main attraction is their
intertextuality. Meek (1988) has commented on the great value of texts like
The Jolly Postman (Ahlberg,1986) and *Each Peach Pear Plum* (Ahlberg, 1981)
for creating a shared culture in a classroom as children enjoy recognising
characters from other well known stories. However, teachers need to be aware
that these texts can present a particular challenge for children who are new to
English and less familiar with traditional English rhymes and tales.

Source text and target language in dual language books

While many of the decisions that translators of children's literature make apply equally to dual language books, there is a marked difference between both forms of publication in the way they handle the relationship between source and target language. For the translator working in a dual language format, the adequacy/acceptability debate has to be conducted well before the work of translation begins. Because the two texts are presented in parallel in dual language books, whatever alterations are made to the translation have to be made to both texts.

Shavit's first principle, that 'translators adjust the text for what is considered 'good for the child", has to apply at the level of choice of text. Publishers seek texts that will achieve the cross cultural aim of representing different cultures in an authentic and positive manner while ensuring that ethnic and gender stereotyping is avoided.

Shavit's second principle: 'translators adjust the text to a child's ability to read and comprehend' presents more difficult decisions for translators as they need to aim for broadly equivalent levels of readability in both languages. With respect to comprehension of cultural content, given that one of the purposes of the books is to introduce children to different cultures, the books generally retain the original names of characters, places and other cultural artefacts referred to in the text. As most of the texts are picture books, the illustrations can support the understanding of many unfamiliar terms. The reader of the *Swirling Hijab* (Robert, 2002) can infer from the pictures what a *hijab* is. Some books provide a glossary to explain terms that may be un-familiar.

Children reading the books are most likely to be doing so because they are proficient in one language but not the other, or indeed because they are semi-proficient in both. They may be aiming to understand a text used in English in the classroom through reading it in their home language. The children who feature in the research described in this book were using the books in the opposite direction. Able to read English in varying degrees, they were learning to read Albanian, Urdu, Turkish, French and Gujarati. In the case of Lek and Durkan (Chapter 7), while they could decode the text in both Turkish and English, they struggled to understand fully its meaning in both languages.

In all of these case studies, the children were using, in various ways, both texts on the page simultaneously. Edwards and Walker (*op cit*:342) have noted the importance of the translation faithfully mirroring the original text. This close match across both languages is essential as the inexperienced readers who use the books seek to understand a word or a phrase in one language by finding the equivalent in the other. A more experienced reader, such as Albana, can be interested in the fact that, in *Handa's Hen* (Browne, 2002), for example, three alliterating words in English, 'hurried and scurried and skipped' are translated by only one in Albanian: *kërcyer*. However a less experienced reader like Mydda is confused when reading *The Two Cats* in Urdu and English, by the difference between the Urdu text which describes Mother Hubbard feeding God's creatures and the English which specifies that she fed her cats (Chapter 6).

The fact that the books are used in this way makes it difficult for translators to capture the spirit of the original text through using equivalent, but different, metaphors, jokes and word play. This creates a limiting factor. Canonical texts with elaborate word play, rhyme, rhythm and alliteration are likely to lose a great deal in translation because of the requirement to stay close to the letter of the work. The more literary qualities the original text has, the more challenging the translation task will become. The commercial pressure to translate one English text into up to two dozen different languages compounds the problem and may be one reason why publishers who work in this way often commission specially written or adapted texts which avoid stylistic features that are hard to translate.

Out of a sample of ten dual language story books in French and English picked at random off a library shelf, seven appeared to have been written specifically for multiple translation. Only one of these, *A Journey through Islamic Arts* (Robert, 2005), presented a sophisticated and elegant style in both languages. Of the remaining nine texts, all interesting and attractive stories, not one presented the challenges that canonical children's literature is likely to offer through use of rhythmic or rhyming language, metaphor, slang or dialect. These non-canonical texts appeared to have been chosen to be accessible to children of approximately the same age and level of reading skill for all the languages into which they were translated, and to meet the cultural and moral standards expected of texts aimed at young children in school.

The relationship between source and target language is only one of the language-related issues facing the translator. Many other complex operational decisions have to be made.

Language choice, language variety and register in dual language books

In Chapter 2 the discussion of language stressed the importance of teachers knowing about the languages spoken in the homes of their pupils. Where many regional and local languages are spoken, as is common in Africa and the Indian sub-continent, the language of education is likely to be an official language which is substantially different from what many people speak in the home. Young children may not be familiar with this language variety. In this case, using texts in the official language to help them understand English is not effective. They may offer a child a book and a recording in Bengali, only to find that the child speaks Sylheti (a regional language of Bangladesh, widely spoken by the Bangladeshi community in England, but not normally written) in the home and still does not understand the text. Some early productions accompanied books in English and Bengali with the option of both Bengali and Sylheti on tape. Such solutions can be found when books are produced for a local and well identified population. Multimedia resources such as CD ROMs and Talking Pens are well equipped to provide several audio versions to match any given text.

Stylistic norms for children's literature vary greatly from language to language. The extent to which the standard form of the language is expected in children's books and slang and dialects are accepted varies from culture to culture. Shavit has commented on how a high literary style is expected in translations into Hebrew as children's literature has to be explicitly 'educationally good' and is seen as providing an opportunity to improve children's vocabulary (1986). The mothers of Magda and Albana (see Chapter 5) reacted with shock when offered a French and Albanian dual language story, *Les Neuf Frères et le Diable* (Bajraktari, 2003) which had been translated into Geg, a Kosovan dialect of Albanian, presumably to ensure it was understood by speakers of that dialect, but which the women considered to be quite unsuitable for use in a published text. O'Connell (1999), who translates from German to Irish, has noted that there can be particular issues when texts are translated from a major to a lesser-used language. This is a familiar situation for users of dual language books in community languages in the UK. The formal literary Gujarati of the *Raja's Big Ears* story (Desai, 1989) caused difficulties for children brought up in the UK with limited access to literacy in that language (Sneddon and Patel, 2003).

Teachers, parents and teaching assistants who use dual languages books have to be prepared to engage with the debate about the appropriateness of a translation for their particular children. Some argue that there is little point in translating a text into the home language if the children still don't understand it because it is too formal. An example of this is the mother who complained about the use of the very literary *vrux* ('tree' in Gujarati) in the *Raja's Big Ears*, instead of the more common *jhaad*. Others, like Mohamed's mother in the present study, were delighted to find the word *vrux* used. She argued that the whole point of reading in Gujarati to her children was to teach them 'the language of books'. As well as the choice of language variety and register for the main body of the target text, translators may be faced with expressions in dialect and slang incorporated into the source text, for which equivalents have to be found in the target language that will have the same social and cultural connotations.

While publishers of texts produced for a wider market will generally translate into the standard form of the language, the translations into south Asian languages of an canonic text such as *The Very Hungry Caterpillar* (Carle, 1992) is full of English words, either because the translations for foods such as salami are not available or because the English words, such as apple, are the ones commonly used by the target audience.

Once the issue of language register and variety has been decided, the main challenges still remain for the translator: rendering the meaning in a language with a very different structure.

Issues in language structure

The structure and grammatical conventions of different languages create a whole new layer of operational decisions for translators. For example, when translating from English into a language that uses grammatical gender, decisions have to be made about the sex of animals and the cultural connotations of making this explicit in the target text when it may have been left deliberately ambiguous in the source (O'Connell,1999). Children who are much more fluent in English than in their home language can find issues of gender really challenging (Sneddon and Patel, 2003) as did Mydda when she encountered the Urdu rhyme *bander, bandriya* (male monkey, female monkey). When translating from English into languages that use different forms of address according to status and relationship, decisions have to be made about the position of characters with respect to each other which may have been left unspecified in the original text. Such decisions can change the social and cultural impact of the text.

One of Shavit's key principles was concerned with comprehension. The content of a story will generally determine the age group of the children at whom it is aimed and this needs to be matched to an appropriate level of readability in both languages. Puurtinen has noted that, while particular grammatical structures may occur in both the source and the target language, it may not be appropriate to translate them directly, as they may have a different distribution in the target language, making the text less accessible (1994). Sarah, for example, whose reading in French is reported in Chapter 8, struggled with the *passé simple*, a past tense widely used in print but less commonly in everyday speech.

Lathey notes 'The aural texture of a translation is of paramount importance to a child still engaged in discovering the power of language' (2006:10). Children's books are commonly read to young children by adults and the rhythmic qualities of the text can bring the best children's texts close to poetry in their patterning of language. While this makes the translation of texts which use rhyme and alliteration particularly challenging, translators must bear in mind that all texts for children should pass a reading aloud test to be enjoyed by readers and listeners.

Cultural choices in the translation of children's literature
Cultural issues in translated literature

As described above, different cultural values and ways of socialising children are reflected in the cultural norms and the expectations of texts written for children in any given society. In the introduction to a reader on the translation of children's literature, Lathey defines this as '...the transposition of a children's text from one language and culture to another reflects differing expectations and interpretations of childhood' (2006:2).

Different traditions, formats and genres produce different expectations: the use of repetition in the text, a requirement for a happy ending, a strong and explicit moral message, the avoidance of certain topics (common ones being sex and death). Certain cultures have literary strengths in particular genres. The recent worldwide success of English authors such as Rowling, Tolkien, Pullman and C.S. Lewis has demonstrated the great strength of the tradition of fantasy in English literature for children. Children's literature in French is particularly creative in the field of the *bande dessinée* (cartoon narrative) and the *Tintin* and *Astérix* series are known internationally.

The bulk of dual language books in England is bought by schools and, specifically, by schools that have a commitment to multicultural education and therefore to challenging racist and xenophobic attitudes as well as promoting equality. There is currently much public debate about what constitutes core

British values. Perhaps our choice of literature for children best demonstrates the values to which we aspire. While teachers, especially of older children, may welcome controversial material in children's books as a starting point for classroom debate, many primary teachers avoid introducing material into the school that does not match its ethos. They assume that children and their families will consider that books available in school and the attitudes that are represented in them meet with the school's approval.

While one of the main purposes of producing translated literature for children is to introduce them to different cultures, the requirement to meet acceptable cultural norms limits the range available. Texts written at a time when norms were different become unacceptable because they promote stereotypes and pejorative language that were part of the culture at the time of writing. For example, a recent translation of Hergé's *Tintin in the Congo*, from the French text written in 1931, (Hergé, 2005) features stereotypes which are no longer acceptable and led to the book being withdrawn from a number of bookshops (Knight, 2007).

Traditional stories for children published in India have been used by English teachers who take advantage of the fact that the same story book is generally available in several of the main Indian languages as well as English. The official multilingual status of India ensures that popular texts are routinely translated. Particularly popular in English schools have been *Rupa the Elephant* (Patel, 1974), for example, and the *Woman and the Crow* (Shankar, 1981) and animal fables. Other traditional Indian tales travel less well to a multicultural Britain.

Sharing culture through dual language books

With the aim of reflecting authentic culture in London communities, Gregory and Penman and Jennie Ingham used drama and writing workshops with parents, story tellers and artists to produce versions of stories such as *The Fisherman and his Wife* (Gregory and Penman, 1985) and the *Naughty Mouse* (Stone, 1989). When traditional stories are told from memory there is no author whose text must be respected. This leaves great scope to interpret and shape the stories to meet the needs of the multicultural audience of English school children. The aim is to produce stories that will introduce children to new cultures and values, through providing positive representations of characters and situations. Tales can be discarded or significantly adapted if they reinforce gender stereotypes or have negative representations of people from other cultures or of people with disabilities. The *Naughty Mouse* is a lively and enjoyable tale but the mouse was not thought, at the time of publication, to present a suitable role model for children, getting away as he did with bullying and extortion (Amanda Welch, 2009).

The stories developed in the projects mentioned above created a space in the classroom in which cultures could be shared. While the stories chosen for translation represented a particular language and culture, many were translated into the languages most widely spoken by children in London schools at the time. Gregory's and Penman's stories, grouped around the theme of 'wishing tales' were published with the clear intention of enabling '... teachers, parents and children to share traditional tales from their differing cultures, and to encourage and reinforce children's bilingualism' (1985: cover). Jennie Ingham associates published their stories with a similar intention. The adoption of a single story, chosen as being of interest to young children and representing the values of the multicultural classroom, translated into a wide range of languages used in the UK, has been adopted by commercial publishers, such as Milet and most notably Mantra Lingua, the largest commercial publisher of children's dual language materials.

Stories reinterpreted in this way can travel well but some are greatly transformed in the journey across cultures. An example of this occurs in the *Raja's Big Ears* (Desai, 1989). In Desai's version, Manji the barber is troubled by trying to keep the secret of the Raja's ears, and goes into the jungle 'to think in peace and quiet'. In the original Gujarati story (Gijubhai, 1973) the barber's stomach is churning with anxiety and he *pachi e disha e jawa gayo* (went to the toilet, literally 'the woods'). The moral of the Gijubhai story is that one should never confide a secret to a barber. The whole Desai story is an interesting example of a transfer of values from one culture to another in a children's story. Gone, in the Desai version, is the curse on the king for killing sparrows, which made his ears as big as winnowing frames. The moral of the Desai story is that the king is loved and respected by his subjects for being kind and fair and he learns to appreciate that this is much more important than the size of his ears (Sneddon and Patel, 2003). A moral message much more in keeping with the values of the multicultural classroom.

Conclusion

Translation is a fascinating but daunting task. Dual language books present many opportunities for all children to learn new languages and for bilingual children in particular to learn new words and turns of phrase, to work in groups to discuss the words chosen and their implications and to suggest preferred alternatives. This is an activity that is particularly suited to community language schools whose pupils will be familiar to varying extents with both languages. However, translation can only provide a flavour of the meaning of the original text. Teachers need to be aware of these limitations: no translation is likely to satisfy all readers.

Both the research and the experience of practitioners suggest that the more successful bilingual books are carefully targeted at their intended audience. This implies that there is much to be gained from a close relationship between publishers and teachers who are, at the time of writing, the prime users of the books. The teachers who met at the University of East London from 2002 to 2004 were researching the use of multilingual materials in their classrooms, evaluating responses from children, parents and colleagues, sharing this information with Mantra Lingua and, in so doing, had some impact on materials offered in the publisher's catalogue.

Those who read aloud to children, whether parents or teachers, develop the skill to adapt the language of the text to the audience, to abridge, expand, explain, substitute and engage children in the narrative. Used in this way, dual language texts have much to offer; skilled readers have been known to engage a whole class in a narrative in a language they do not know, and teach them to watch and listen for clues and respond to the rhythm and patterns of the language used.

5
Magda and Albana

When I first meet Magda and Albana, they are 6 years old. They were born in Britain of Albanian parents and are in Year 1 at school. They are best friends, and so are their mothers, Miranda and Lere. They have been learning to read in Albanian with their mothers for six months and are enthusiastic and proud of their skills. The original research plan was to observe them reading for four sessions, three towards the end of the summer term and a fourth in the autumn. However, the group are keen to maintain a more informal contact with the researcher and so this part of the study offers an opportunity for a longer view of the girls' developing biliteracy, charting their move from reading into writing and noting significant developments in their cultural identity over a period of two and a half years.

The context
The *Developing Reading Skills through Home Languages Project* of the London Borough of Redbridge that was set up in the Spring of 2006 provided an ideal opportunity for making contact with children and parents who were using dual language books to learn to read (EMAT, 2007). I was invited to visit two of the schools in which the project took place. Navneet Padda was a teacher in a Year 1 class in which the majority of children were bilingual. She was herself a bilingual in Punjabi and English and was keen to encourage children to use their own languages in the classroom. She used dual language books to teach reading in English and offered advice and support to parents to read the same books with their children in the language of the home. Children were given books and CDs to take home. The use of these books enabled Padda to discuss the children's reading experiences and progress in the classroom even though she knew only one (Punjabi) of the nine home languages spoken by the children.

Miranda and Lere had only one book each in Albanian at home and greatly valued the dual language books offered by the school as the only resource available for teaching children. They felt culturally isolated as there were few other Albanian families in the neighbourhood at the time. At our first meeting the girls talked excitedly about an Albanian concert they had attended. The women explained that there were Albanian organisations but that they were far away in central London.

Language and literacy experiences at home

While Miranda and Lere discuss the difficulties of maintaining fluency in Albanian as children become dominant in English, Magda enjoys the task of completing a visual representation of her language use in the home. As she draws pictures and colours in the arrows, she introduces her family and explains:

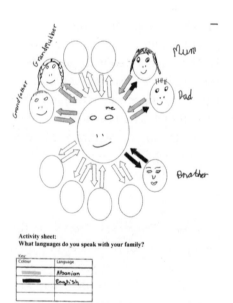

Activity sheet:
What languages do you speak with your family?

Key:

Colour	Language
	Albanian
	English

Magda's language use at home

That's me, that's my Mum, that's my Dad, that's my Grandma, that's my Grandfather and that's my brother. His name is Adi. I talk to my Daddy a bit in English, a lot in Albanian and my Dad talks a lot in Albanian. My Mum talks half English and half Albanian... no. I talk to my Mum and she talks to me always Albanian. And my grandparents, always Albanian because they don't know English. My brother, I talk to him in English and he talks to me in English.

Magda proceeds to explain that she was born in London and will be visiting Albania in August. She spoke mainly Albanian until she started school when she recalls 'I didn't speak really well English'. But she remembers that 'people were helpful' and does not feel that this was a difficult time. Her mother confirms that Magda learnt English very quickly. Although Magda's diagram suggests that she speaks quite a lot of Albanian to her parents, Miranda is worried that her use of the language is declining as she becomes more proficient and literate in English.

Albana explains her diagram:

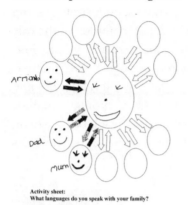

Activity sheet:
What languages do you speak with your family?

Albana's language use at home
'My Dad, I speak English and Albanian and Dad the same, and Mummy. My brother, I speak English. He doesn't know Albanian, he can't talk Albanian. He is very small, he is four and a half.'

Lere reports that Albana, like her friend, learned to speak English quickly when she started playgroup. Like Miranda, she expresses great concern that Albana's use of Albanian declined dramatically after she started school. While she and her husband always speak Albanian together, she also likes to speak English to Albana to improve her own skills.

Albana's mother is delighted that, since the beginning of the project, she is speaking much more Albanian at home. She comments that, through learning to read, 'she has learned words in Albanian that I don't know'. Miranda has noted a similar effect with Magda. This increased use appears to be reflected in the girls' current estimate of their language use. The girls have made friends readily at school but it is only to each other that they can speak Albanian. While their mothers greatly welcome the dual language books provided by the school, it is the girls who maintain the momentum of the project, insisting that their busy mothers find time to read with them.

Learning to read in Albanian

By the time I meet the girls it is late June and they are near the end of Year 1. They have been reading with their mothers in Albanian for six months. Their teacher reports that, from needing support to read with understanding in English at the beginning of the year, they have both emerged into the group of top readers in their class. She is convinced that their developing biliteracy is a factor in this success.

The first three recorded sessions were close together at the end of that first year. As the girls read a selection of dual language books, their strategies and those of their mothers emerged. While there is much in common in the way the mothers help their daughters and the girls' responses, it is also obvious that they have different learning styles and different strengths. Both mother-daughter pairs have a preference for reading the same text several times and the purpose of this strategy becomes apparent as the recordings progress. Magda and Albana are both good readers in English and the following section explores how they use their skills to decode Albanian text and the strategies they use to make meaning.

Working out the words

Magda explains to me 'The Albanian alphabet has got more letters than English because it has 36 letters'. In fact there are only two letters which look visually different from English ones: ë (sounds 'ee') and the less common ç. Letters such as q, j and y represent different phonemes in Albanian, and there are a number of digraphs (which teachers of Albanian call 'letters' in English) such as fj, dh, ng, xh.

Miranda and Lere compare learning to read in English with learning in Albanian and discuss the very different challenges. Lere is not the first person to find that the irregularity of English presents a challenge, although she notes that many common English words are short. Reading in Albanian is easier because of the close relationship between sounds and letters, Lere explains, but there are many long words with a complex structure and children have trouble placing the stress in the right position. Both women started by teaching their daughters the different sound values of letters in Albanian and Magda recalls how her mother helped her to work out new words by using fridge magnets.

Magda reading

Magda's first choice for reading is the beautifully illustrated *The Swirling Hijab* (Robert, 2002). The book is new to her. She starts reading the Albanian text, decoding slowly and cautiously, blending sounds as she reads, glancing at her mother for confirmation. Miranda offers 'mmm' when she is right and whispers the correct pronunciation when she is stuck:

> Magda: (reading title page) *perçja valos..*
>
> Miranda: *valez...*
>
> Magda: valëzuese (*The swirling hijab*) *perçja e mamit tim është e zezë e butë dhe e ja, je*

Miranda: (whispers) *gjerë*

Magda: *gjerë* (my mum's hijab is black and soft and wide) *jë* ...

Miranda: (whispers) *fortesë për* ...

Magda: *fortesë për mua që të fshi... fshikem brenda* (a fort for me to hide inside) *është* ...

Miranda: mmm

Magda: *si ve... ve... velat e një an...*

Miranda: *anijeje*

Magda: *anijeje që valo...*

Miranda: (whispers) *valëviten*

Magda: *valëviten*

Miranda: mmm

Magda: *në ajër* (a ship's sails flapping in the air)

Miranda: mmm (sounds very encouraging)

Magda: *një ngushel* ...

Miranda: *ngushëllim*

Magda (gaining in speed and confidence): *ngushëlim për mua kur mami nuk është pranë* (a comforter when she's not there)

Magda is entirely focused on the Albanian text throughout that first reading and only asks two questions about meaning. Her mother provides whispered support to avoid interrupting the flow of her reading. Magda has not yet looked at the English text. When asked to explain briefly what she has read, there is a long silence. Then she reads the first English sentence 'My Mum's hijab is black and soft and wide' and she explains 'hijab is *perçja* and black is *është*': She proceeds to read faultlessly the rest of the English text.

Albana reading

Albana's reading style is very different. She has brought *Handa's Hen* (Browne, 2002), but, unlike Magda, this is not a first reading as she has looked at the book the night before with her mother. Her voice is soft but her pronunciation is very clear and she reads with confidence.

> Albana: *Gjyshja e Handës kishte një pulë të zëzë. Emrin e kishte Mondi – dhe çdo mëngjes Handa i jepte Mondit dicka për të ngrënë.* (Handa's Grandma had one black hen. Her name was Mondi – and every morning Handa gave Mondi her breakfast.)

When she encounters dialogue in the next page, more expression comes into her voice and she calls out '*O gjyshe!*' (Grandma!) in a loud voice. '*A e ke parë Mondin?*' (Can you see Mondi?).

Niele corrects her pronunciation of *flutura* (butterfly) and *laramanë* (stripey) where she gets the stress wrong. By the time she reaches page 5 of the text she is beginning to encounter strange animal names and more unfamiliar words. Her reading slows down as she decodes carefully and self corrects.

> Albana: *Ato panë prapa disa enëve prej arg... argjile.* (They peeped behind some clay pots.) *Pesë zo.. zogj të bukura... të bukur, tha Akeyo.* (Five beautiful sunbirds, said Akeyo.)

She is now reading cautiously, syllable by syllable, carefully blending phonemes: *nën..të..gar..gun..jë të shndit..shëm* (nine shiny starlings). With the repetitive cry of the chicks on page 13, Albana recovers her confidence and enjoys cheeping softly with expression *ciu, ciu, ciu, ciu*. She proceeds to read the story faultlessly in English and Lere checks she knows the word for mice, *minj*, which she has mispronounced as *min*. Albana explains to her mother what 'grain' and 'stripey' mean and that *hardhuca* are lizards in English.

Albana is very assured in her reading and even when decoding unfamiliar words she maintains a good intonation in both languages but, like Magda, she is not keen to talk about the story. At this stage in the reading, also like Magda, she has kept both languages separate, reading through the whole story in Albanian first, then in English. Navmeet Padda, her teacher, was present as an observer for part of this session, and commented on Albana's different pronunciation of the name Handa, depending on which language she was reading.

Reading the text twice

Magda also likes *Handa's Hen* and reads it for the first time in the second observation session. As before with *The Swirling Hijab*, she struggles at first with decoding.

> Magda (on page 3 of the text): *Handa dhe Akeyo pan*
> Miranda: *panë*
> Magda: *pane rreth ko...*
> Miranda: *kotecit*
> Magda: *kotecit të...*
> Miranda: *pulave*
> Magda: *pulave*

She declines to retell the story. Her focus on word-by-word decoding does not yet provide her with a confident understanding of what she has read on her first reading. Miranda asks: 'do you understand the story? Magda: 'not too much'. She brings the book back to the third session before the summer break. This time she reads the Albanian followed by the English page by page. On this second attempt, she reads with speed, confidence and expression:

Magda:

> *Gjyshja e Handës kishte një pulë të zezë. Emrin e kishte Mondi – dhe çdo mëngjes Handa I jepte Mondit dicka për të ngrënë.* Handa's grandma had one black hen. Her name was Mondi – and every morning Handa gave Mondi her breakfast.
>
> *Një ditë, Mondi nuk erdhi për të ngrënë. O Gjyshe, thirri Handa. A e ke parë Mondin? Jo, that Gjyshja. Por kam parë shoqen tënde. Akeyo! tha Handa. Më ndihmo ... me ndhimo ta gjej Mondin.* One day, Mondi didn't come for her food. Grandma! called Handa. Can you see Mondi? No, said Grandma. But I can see your friend. Akeyo! said Handa, help me find Mondi.

Magda reads almost faultlessly through the first half of the book and needs correcting only with *laramanë*, when she struggles with the position of the stress.

Making meaning together – Magda

Miranda moves away from her role as the whispering prompter and starts asking questions. 'What is *gëlltitur*?'

Magda immediately answers 'swallow'.

Miranda: are there any words, Magda, that you don't know?

Magda: euh, *Gjysha*?

Miranda: *Gjysha* is grandma. What about *shoqen*?

Magda: Handa's friend.

Miranda: do you know what *ndihmo*?

Magda: *ndihmo* means help me.

Miranda: good girl, Magda!

Up to this point issues of meaning are simple as Miranda knows the answer. When it comes to the exotic animals, while the words may be unfamiliar in both languages, the illustrations are very supportive and Magda knows how to use them. However, Miranda is not fully fluent in English and a number of instances occur in which she is unsure how to explain the word.

For example, in *The Swirling Hijab* (on page 9) Magda reads: *mateli i një mbre...*

> Miranda: *mbretëresche*. That says queen.
>
> Magda: mm?
>
> Miranda: queen!
>
> Magda: *mbretëresche luftare...*
>
> Miranda: *luftëtare...*
>
> Magda: *luftëtare*?
>
> Miranda: *luftëtare*. Um... it's like...
>
> She looks at Lere who suggests: is it like a fighter?
>
> Miranda: yes, it's strong...
>
> Together, with Magda, they look at the English text
>
> Magda: it's 'warrior', yes...

In *Handa's Hen*, Magda has read on page 3: *Handa dhe Akeyo pane rreth kotecit te pulave* ... as above. Miranda has spotted one of the very few words in this book that is similar in both languages. She asks: *fluturojnë*, it's very similar, Albanian and English. Do you know what it is?

Miranda: 'it's when the butterflies are fluttering'. She demonstrates flapping wings. Then she asks a harder question: *rreth kotecit*?

> Magda: mmm...
>
> Miranda: *kotecit*, around, around hunted. Do you know English hunted?
>
> Magda: yeah
>
> Miranda: can you explain?
>
> Magda: it's when, it's like you go somewhere and you look for, like when you go shopping... and they were hunting, to look for Han... Mondi
>
> Miranda: no. Hunted is, it means, Magda, when a house, when the hen stays, leaving, they hunted around
>
> Magda: they are looking for Mondi
>
> Miranda: I use for looking around the house, yes

Magda and Miranda seem to have negotiated their way into understanding the meaning of the word that is relevant to the text.

Towards the end of the book, on page 15, Magda reads: *u kthen me vrap dhe duke kërcyer, tek Gjyshja...* (translated in the book as 'hurried and scurried and skipped back to Grandma's...'). Lere has been following Magda's reading and comments: 'There's a lot of new words there. We haven't heard them.'

Miranda, pointing to the Albanian text: 'this is one (word) and the translation is different. Yes, the translation is not, is doesn't go in the words'

Lere: 'different words, different way'

Miranda: 'Albanian has one word, *kërcyer,* English are three'

This is the first time they have commented on a difference between the two texts. At the end of her second reading of *Handa's Hen*, Magda volunteers to retell the story in Albanian which she does successfully.

Negotiating meaning – Albana

Albana loves the story of *Not Again, Red Riding Hood* (Clynes and Daykin, 2003) which tells of a new adventure of Red Riding Hood who meets characters from traditional stories as she takes some cookies to her father in the forest.

On the second observational session she brings the book which she has, as before, read once with her mother. She reads alternative pages. Her reading in Albanian is slow and cautious; in English, lively and full of expression. However she is much more focused on meaning than last time she read. After reading on page1:

> Albana: *kësulëkuqja ishte akoma pak e frikësuar nga ideja se duhej të hynte në pyll përsëri* (Now Red Riding Hood still felt a bit nervous about going into the wood). What is *akoma?*
>
> Lere: *akoma* means 'yet' in English
>
> Albana and Lere look for 'yet' in the English text and don't find it.
>
> Lere: still. It's similar. I was trying to remember 'still' and I couldn't. It didn't come in my mind. But it's the same, it's similar. Anything else you don't understand in English?
>
> Albana: *hynte*
>
> Lere: *hynte.* It means to get in. For get inside for example, or to get in the forest, go in the forest

Lere proceeds to explain that, although Albana can decode text and read with expression she has difficulty understanding the less familiar language of the book.

> I have tried with her to translate you know, sentences, but she can do the short ones and not the long ones. But as we are just making them separate, two parts of the sentence, you know. I try to do the whole sentence with her but it's very hard. She told me 'Mummy can you please break it up because I don't

understand and I can't say all of it.' So I just took part of the sentence and we could do it. She can't translate many words, or even to explain in Albanian, to make her understand.

The position of the two texts varies in this book, the Albanian sometimes first, sometimes the English. Albana reads through the book as it comes. The next page she reads has the English on one page and the Albanian on the next.

Albana: her Mum counted ten freshly make cookies into a basket. Two, four, six, eight, ten. Red Riding Hood gave her Mum a big hug and off she went. *Mami numëroi dhejë biskota te sapopjekura dhe i futi në shporte.*

Miranda interrupts to point out a spelling error in the book: 'some words is not writing well.'

Lere agrees: 'it is, letters missing in the words, but I just explained to Albana. Can you say this sentence in English Albana?'

Albana (who has see the English text on the previous page), slowly: Mum counted ten ... biscuits ...

Lere: what about *sapopjekura*? Just try to remember. *Sapopjekura*, it means she has just cooked the biscuits at that moment. They are very nice and hot. O.K.

Albana: *kësulëkuqja e përqafoi mamin duke e shtrënguar fort dhe iku.*

Lere: what is that in English? What does it mean *e përqafoi*?

Albana: . ...

Lere (prompting): to give...

Albana: to give a hug

Lere: to give Mummy a hug. It means *përqafoi* it means to give a hug. What about *shtrënguar*?

Albana (demonstrating): she holded her Mummy very, very ... tight!

Lere (laughing): she gave Mummy a big hug! Tight and very... To give a hug like this, does it mean to tight or what does that mean? To squeeze? Gave her a big hug and squeeze her.

On the next page Albana reads: *kam shumë kohë që jam mbyllur në këtë kullë dhe po vdes urie.*

Lere asks: *po vdes urie*? What does that mean in English?

Albana: hungry.

Lere: yes, when you are very very hungry. You are starving. Your tummy needs food! What about *kam shumë hohë që jam ...*' Can you say it in English? *Kam shumë hohë?*

Albana: ....

Lere: I have been stuck in this tower... mm?

Lere is using a fairly common teacherly style, explaining, asking a lot of questions, and not always allowing time for an answer. She has been very anxious about Albana's decreasing use of Albanian and is trying to break down the task for her. She explains:

> It is hard for her. I want to find the best way for her to understand it. But I think it is more easy for her in English, even if it's the wrong way: it's better to explain in Albanian. To make it easier for her, we use both languages. But for her it is easier in English.

Although Lere and Miranda have different ways of teaching the girls; with Lere doing a lot of explaining and Miranda more inclined to prompt, both girls develop a confident reading style over those first three sessions and, when they have had more than one opportunity to read a text, are confident about retelling the story.

After the summer break, during which both girls went on holiday to Albania and spoke the language the whole time with their extended families, there is a noticeable shift in their skills. At the fourth and final formal observation session in November, Albana brings *Lima's Red Hot Chilli* (Mills, 2000) and reads it fluently and with expression in both languages, announcing 'there are no hard words!' She explains that the only words she has asked about are *arrë kokosi ngjyrë* (brown coconut). When offered a completely new book, *Fox Fables* (Casey, 2006), she reads it carefully in Albanian, with a few prompts from her mother and then proceeds to tell the story in English, getting stuck only because she doesn't know the English word for *lejlekun* (crane).

Magda had brought her own book of children's short stories entirely in Albanian, bought while on holiday. To show off her skill, she chooses to read one she has not tried before. There is a full page of text with only one illustration and a lot of long words. Miranda supports with the occasional prompt:

Magda: *Më në fund ka ardhur pranvera! Dimri I ashpër sh..*

Miranda: *shkoi*

Magda: *Shkoi e iku! Ajri është më I ngrohtë dhe dielli na guda ...*

Miranda: *na gudulis*

Magda: *Na gudulis I drojtur fytyrën*

When she has finished reading she explains:

It's about when the girl goes somewhere and it is hot and she likes the place and ... She sees a hedgehog and flowers and a bird with little baby birds and a butterfly and trees and another tree with flowers. It means like because she was waiting and waiting and then it started to be hot...

Learning to write

Before the summer I had suggested to the girls that they might like to try writing a diary in Albanian with help from their mothers and I offered them two hard bound blank books.

At the November session they brought their diaries to show me. I had rather hoped to see a draft which might have provided an indication of how they worked out spelling in Albanian, but both girls were far too professional to offer this. Both had drafted in Albanian, received help from their mothers with spelling and then copied their text in perfect handwriting. They produced the books side by side for me to photograph.

As Albana and Magda translated their diary entries for my benefit, I suggested to them that they might like to make their own dual language books based on their holiday experiences. The girls liked the idea but both expressed concern that their pictures would not be good enough. We agreed to meet again the following Spring to discuss drafts and work out how the books could be presented and reproduced. The school's Ethnic Minority Achievement co-ordinator, Catherine Coop, supported the project. She suggested that multiple copies could be made for the school library and offered the school's laminating and binding facilities.

Magda's text and pictures were ready by the end of the summer term. She had seen a dual language book produced with Clicker 5 software and had designed her book with a similar layout. She explained that her mother had helped with the Albanian text and that her brother had contributed to the pictures. Albana had produced a full text, but only three pictures. As a perfectionist measuring herself against commercially published books, she was anxious about their quality, but was reassured when she was shown *Maya Sami*, a multilingual book published with children's illustrations (Solbakk, 1994). Both books were ready for proofreading by the Autumn term.

Discussion and further developments

At the point where they started in mainstream school both girls, but Albana in particular, were beginning to lose the active use of Albanian as their English became increasingly fluent. By ensuring support for reading with under-

My grandma was so happy to see us. My Grandma had a big house with a big garden all around the house with lovely and wonderful trees. She used to bake lots of lovely food for us. I felt upset when I saw my Grandma worried because my young uncle had gone to Italy. I had fun when I used to stay with my four aunties and my second auntie's boy. I even liked to stay and play with my third auntie's little girl who was very beautiful and cute. I tried to play with her but she didn't know me.	Gjyshja ime ishte shumë e gezuar qe na shikonte ne. Gjyshja ime kishte një shtepi të madhe me nje kopesht të madh rreth shtepise me shume peme të bukura dhe të mrekullueshme. Ajo kishte pergaditur gjellë shüme të shijshme posacerisht per ne. Unë nuk u ndieva mirë kur shikoja Gjyshen time të merzitur sepse daja im i vogel dhe i vetëm kishte ikur në Italy. Unë u kenaqesha, kur rrinja me kater tezet e mia dhe me dy cunat e tezes se dytë dhe gocen e vogel të tezes së tretë që e dua shumë. Ajo ishte shumë e bukur dhe e ëmbel. Une doja të luaja me ta por ajo nuk më nihte.

Magda's holiday story

Shtëpiq ishte në nje fshat tej vogel në kodar nje shtepi dykateshe e bukur me kopësht te madh me pemë dhe rrala dhe me lule. Gjyshërit, e me u gëzuan shume kur më panë ishte hera e pare dhe më shoqëronin kudo që shkoja dhe me tregonin çdo gjë përreth shtëpisë.

The house was in a small village in the middle of the hills, a beautiful terraced house surrounded by trees with fruit and colourful flowers. Inside my grandparents were very happy when they saw me because it was the first time we met. They followed me everywhere and wanted to show me lots of things around the house.

Albana's holiday story

standing in English and introducing opportunities to learn Albanian, their teacher enabled them to become additive bilinguals with a developing understanding of book language and a widening vocabulary in English and Albanian. Their teacher reported that, by the end of their first year in the main school, the girls were counted among the best readers in the class in English. Albana's mother is delighted 'she knows words in Albanian that I don't know!' The girls had both learned a range of strategies for reading in English which they were able to transfer to learning in Albanian, after their mothers had taught them the basic sound to letter correspondence. The fact that Albanian uses the Roman alphabet and the transparency of the relationship between phonemes and letters enabled them to decode rapidly (Bialystok, 2001; Wyse and Goswami, 2009) and there was never any evidence of confusion between the two phonic systems.

The way in which dual language books were used in class by the teacher created a multilingual and multicultural space in which all children could share personal experiences, be proud of their language skills and explore and develop personal identities. This case study provides a good example of how valuing and using languages and working closely with parents and communities can develop children's confidence in ways suggested by Cummins' empowerment model (1986). Mohammed, whose story is told in Chapter 9, told the researcher 'Magda and Albana talk to each other in Albanian in class'. The invisible sign that says 'English only' had been taken down.

It was obvious from the first encounter with the girls that they were very keen to learn Albanian and were working their way through the school's entire collection of dual language books. Their skills were valued and they were invited to read in assembly. Being biliterate was an important part of their personal identity that they were proud to proclaim and both have expressed their intention to continue developing their skills. During the period of observation, in the long gap between the third and the fourth session, both girls went to Albania on holiday, Albana for the first time. In both their diaries and the stories that developed from them, they write movingly about meeting their grandmothers, the pleasure of playing with their cousins and their regret at leaving at the end of the holiday. During the last observation visit Magda explained she would be performing an Albanian poem in public to celebrate the Albanian national Flag Day. She stood on a chair and declaimed it proudly with actions.

The girls and their mothers felt culturally isolated at the start of the study. During the period of our work together they came into contact with Shpresa (meaning 'hope' in Albanian), an organisation that helped the school to put on a performance of Albanian poetry and dance for refugee week. The success of this performance led to it being presented in several schools. In a further development, the EMA co-ordinator worked with Shpresa to run a lunchtime Albanian club which was popular with the growing number of Albanian children in the school, but also with their friends who came to learn some basic Albanian and enjoyed the dancing. Magda and Albana played a key role in these sessions and Albanian mothers, including Miranda and Lere, took turns at supporting the activities. Albanian culture developed a high profile in the school and was perceived as 'cool' by the children. In the following Spring term the Albanian club was invited to dance at a conference in front of an audience of 120 teachers. Magda and Albana introduced and concluded the proceedings in both English and Albanian with professional confidence and voices that carried to the back of the conference hall.

The stories they wrote with help from their mothers were another great source of pride. They recorded them on a CD, and read them in class. The opportunity arose for Magda to join a weekend complementary Albanian class where her personal book made a great impression.

An additional development was the involvement of Miranda and Lere in school: Miranda worked as a volunteer teaching assistant while attending college and Lere as a trainee nursery assistant, resulting in great improvements in their use of English and starting them off on a professional ladder.

The developments that made such a positive impact on the achievement of Magda and Albana are very much in line with Cummins' empowerment model. They were made possible by teachers who knew how to empower their children: how to interest children in languages, develop biliteracy creatively in the classroom, make use of parents' funds of knowledge, involve community organisations to complement their work and make the best possible use of available resources.

6

The *suraj*, the sun, is inside the *mashriq*, and it comes out

Mydda is 7 and is learning to read in Urdu with her mother. As she moves from reading from a dual language picture book provided by the school to an Urdu primer, a book of illustrated children's rhymes from Pakistan, a difficult dual language text without pictures, and back to a more demanding dual language picture book, her identity as a learner shifts from someone who 'can read, but doesn't like it' in English to a learner who is determined to crack the code in Urdu and who is increasingly excited about and proud of her achievements. Her mother Bismah talks about the family's language and literacy practices and the strategies she deploys to support her daughter.

Context of the school

Half the children in Mydda's east London school are bilingual. The school values the children's linguistic heritage and encourages active bilingualism. An inspection report mentions that 'The school works very successfully to draw on pupils' wide range of backgrounds and cultures' (Ofsted, 2008:2). Displays around the school reflect languages spoken, dual languages books are widely available and bilingual writing and book making workshops are organised for parents. Parents are encouraged to tell stories and read to their children in their home languages.

Language use and literacy practices

Bismah was born in Sialkot, in Pakistan. She is fully bilingual and biliterate in Urdu and English. However she does not speak Urdu to Mydda's father as he is a Punjabi speaker and not fully fluent in Urdu. She has three children. Until the first two were ready to start nursery she spoke both Urdu and English to them at home. She describes how she talked bilingually to the children, teaching them both *bili* and cat for example. She still uses a lot of Urdu to the children at home but, although they understand her, they generally respond in English. When required to, Mydda can speak Urdu to family members in Pakistan on the telephone. The family visit Pakistan periodically and when they do this, Bismah reports that, within a week, Mydda and her brother sound like the local children. Just before our second meeting, young cousins from Pakistan had visited for the whole summer holiday and the children spoke mainly Urdu among themselves. Mydda enjoyed completing a language use diagram. This representation of her complex use of language is reproduced in Chapter 2.

Story telling is an important tradition in Bismah's family's. She recalls her own mother's extensive repertoire of religious, traditional and moral tales as well as her great skill in making up stories on the spot. Bismah herself is a lively story teller and when we first met she was telling Mydda the story of *Chiriya* and *Kawa*, which she translated as the *Sparrow and the Crow*, a cautionary tale about why one should not steal. Mydda listened intently. It was clear that, whatever her own reluctance to speak Urdu, Mydda followed it with pleasure. Bismah explained that she does not encourage the watching of television: 'I prefer the children to read'.

Multilingual literacies in the home

Bismah has some Urdu books at home. She is fond of poetry and children's rhymes. She has books of religious stories, but she explains that they are written for children brought up in Pakistan and are too advanced for her children. She borrows Urdu books from the public library and, when reading stories to the children, simplifies them where necessary to ensure they understand.

Religious education is important to Bismah's family. Mydda started learning the Qur'an and some writing in Arabic with her older brother when she was three and a half years old with a private teacher who came to her home. Bismah would like the children to learn to read and write both languages with understanding. However, concerned that the children may become confused by the similarities and differences between the Arabic and Urdu scripts, Bismah put off teaching the children Urdu until recently. She comments that, while Mydda can be forgetful and has a short attention span for reading, she pronounces Urdu well and has good handwriting.

Brown Bear, Brown Bear, what do you see?

This is the book, in Urdu and English, Mydda chose on the first recorded session with her mother. The book is familiar to her from nursery. The choice seems to be a good one: this is one of the 'texts that teach' which, according to Margaret Meek (1988), strongly support inexperienced readers. The repetitive structure of the text together with the clear illustrations make it easy for the reader to memorise phrases, guess animal names and understand the story.

> Brown bear, Brown bear, what do you see?
> *booray baloo, booray baloo, toomay kya nazar aa raha hai*
> I see a red bird looking at me.
> *Mujay ek surkh cheerya nazar aa rahi hai mujay deekhti hoi.*
> (Martin, 2004: 1)

The same dialogue is repeated on each page with a different coloured animal featured.

Bismah reads first in Urdu, one word at a time, Mydda follows. Bismah covers up the English text on the second page and asks Mydda to translate the Urdu: 'what is he saying here?' Mydda responds 'I can see a bird.' When asked to read on, Mydda guesses from the illustrations and Bismah asks her to 'look at it and try to read it, not guess it.' Mydda reads *pilee batak* (yellow duck) but then guesses the next word. Bismah objects:

> where's *mujay*? (I) I can't see any *meem* (the Urdu name of the letter that sounds *m*). How can you say *mujay*? You're not trying to read it, are you? It's *toomay* (you). I know, it's a bit difficult this word, but if you break the letters and try to sound them out like you do in English, it will be easier.

Bismah sounds out the phrase *toomay kya nazar aa raha hai*? (what do you see?).

Bismah and Mydda are very intent. The extract above demonstrates some of the strategies that Bismah deploys: reading and repetition, translation into English to check understanding, encouraging the breaking down of words into sounds, providing clues. As she works her way through the book, guessing some words from the pictures, it becomes apparent that Mydda's knowledge of colours and animal names in Urdu is fairly limited. She knows that *hara* is green, but not that *mendek* is a frog. She has forgotten that *bandar* is a monkey until her mother prompts 'you saw it in the zoo the other day, jumping and dancing' and provides the first sound, b. Bismah reminds her daughter to use environmental print: 'what's brown in Urdu? You have got all of them written in your class, English and Urdu. You don't read them. I tell you to keep reading them. It's *booray baloo* (brown bear)'.

In spite of her reported short attention span, Mydda is strongly engaged with the challenge presented to her and is keen to read the whole book. She is transferring what she knows about reading this kind of text in English to work out the meaning in Urdu. While she can guess a great deal from illustrations and repetition, she begins to follow her mother's request to pay more attention to initial letters. She gradually gains in confidence and, by the time she gets to the goldfish on page 17, she is able to work out *sunehri matcheli, sunehri matcheli, toomay kya nazar aa raha hai* (goldfish, goldfish, what do you see?) with a minimum of help.

The challenge of the script

As suggested by Bialystok's work on the nature of transfer between languages (2001), the Urdu script offers Mydda a much greater challenge than that faced by the Albanian, French or Turkish readers in the study. While she is familiar with the appearance of the script and its right-to-left directionality from books in the home, Mydda is a beginner at decoding it. There are no visual clues that could link the two systems. Although the regularity of sound to script is much greater in Urdu, the semi-syllabic nature of the script, the diacritics that represent short vowels and the different shapes that letters can take depending on whether they are in initial, medial or final position inside the word, add additional layers of difficulty for the inexperienced reader. Mydda is not able to transfer skills as readily as Albana or Lek.

Books from Pakistan

The session transcribed above took place in July. Events over the summer changed the focus of the sessions. Up to that point, Bismah and Mydda were using the dual language books offered by the school and strategies familiar to both of them from learning to read in English. During the summer holiday Mydda's grandmother came over with her young cousins. She read with Mydda three times a week. The private literacy of the home that, as both Gregory and Kenner have noted, is so rarely familiar to schools, was introduced into the project as Mydda, at our first session after the summer, brought in the colourful Urdu primer she had been using with her grandmother and showed me how it works.

This book has a page for each letter; the sound is illustrated in the traditional manner with a range of objects starting with the letter and some children's rhymes that incorporate the words. Bismah explains how children learn to read in Pakistan 'they learn it more by heart more than they read it, then, when they learn them (the rhymes), they know how to read them'.

Pahlaa Qadam (Arshad, 1999)

Decoding unfamiliar text, that was such a challenge before she had learned her Urdu letters, is now within her reach. Mydda explains that she has read about a third of the book and she starts for me at p1 with the letter which sounds A in Urdu. She reads *a*, *adab* (a greeting), *aam* (a mango). Mydda reads with expression the rhyme that she knows by heart:

> *Alu kachalu mian khahan gaye they, subzi ki tokri me so rahay they, bengun ne laat mari ro pare they, gajar ne payar kya hans pare they.* (Mr potato where have you been? I was sleeping in the vegetable basket, the aubergine kicked me and I started to cry, the carrot comforted me and I started to laugh).

'You see the difference?' comments Bismah, 'from before the holidays and now?'

Mydda proceeds to read pages 2 to 5, with occasional corrections from her mother. She is supported by the illustrations and the fact that all the single words on the page begin with the same letter. She knows all the rhymes by heart which suggests she has read the pages many times. From that session on, Mydda brings the primer and reads a little from it at every session.

Realising how much the rhymes in the primer were helping Mydda, Bismah has brought a favourite book of children's rhymes (Tubassam, 1998) that her sister sent her two years ago and that she has read to the children many times. Mydda starts to read from the first page of a two page poem. Bismah's prompts are frequent and apply to every word in the second line. By the third line, although she is still battling with decoding, Mydda is picking up the strong rhythm of the text. Her mother's prompts are in brackets:

*Bili ko sum jhani aay (chuhay) chuhay (kai) kai (hazar) bazar (hazar)
hazar (hazar means a thousand)*

Bili ne ay (ik) ik bat ne (baat na) na mani.

Rohay (zar) zar o zar

Suno gap shap, suno gap shap

Nao me nani (nadi)nadi doob chali.

*Ma (hathi) hathi (what is a hathi? elephant, hathi ko) hathi ko cha (chunti)
chunti ne (peeta) peeta (chunti: ant).*

(Thousands of mice came to make the cat understand

But she didn't listen to a word

They cried and cried

Listen to the chit chat

Listen to the chit chat

The stream is drowning in the boat

The elephant was beaten by the ant.)

Mydda is keen to complete a reading of the first page and briefly discusses the poem in Urdu with her mother. She is not, however, keen to explain it to me in English.

On my next visit Mydda shows me new pages of the primer she has been working on, but she still struggles to provide an explanation in English. She identifies the letter on page 15 as *ray*, but is unsure, until Bismah confirms, what sound it represents. She reads *roti* correctly, and *radio* and *burj* (pillars) but struggles with *rail*. She works out the rhyme, making a few errors. When I ask her what it means, she becomes shy: 'in the night ... I can't say it!' and she hides behind her mother, 'the trees will be green.' 'No!' says Bismah and prompts her in Urdu. Mydda tries again 'at night it was raining and dark and no one came out'. Bismah laughs and corrects 'and the stars didn't come out.' She draws a little star on the text as a prompt.

On page 16 is another R sound, one that occurs only in a medial position. It's a sound English speaking children find very difficult. Bismah tries again to get Mydda to curl her tongue, roll her R and repeat the word: *rabriwallah* (the pudding man). Mydda decodes the rhyme carefully with help from Bismah and, this time, the words are more familiar and she explains the meaning with confidence: 'when the cat got up the tree, the bird, *cherya*, flew away'.

The next time she brings the primer, she is so keen to read that she starts before I can get the recorder switched on. She is focusing on the letters that represent the contrasting sounds *seen* and *sheen* (page 19). First she reads the headings under the pictures: *suraj* (sun) *saaras* (crane). She decodes carefully *ser-geant* (an English word written in Urdu script). Then she moves straight into reading the text, fluently and confidently: *Suraj mashriq say nikalta hai. Sab ko sukh baant* (the sun rises from the east. It spreads happiness).

Bismah asks: 'Do you know what *suraj* means? Mydda is confident: 'The sun'. 'And *saaya*? 'Shadow'. 'And do you know what *Suraj mashriq say nikalta hai* is? What is *mashriq*?' Mydda doesn't know. Bismah: 'East. *Nikalta he*, what does that mean?' Mydda is keen to show she can explain: 'comes out. The *suraj*, the sun, is inside the *mashriq*, and it comes out.' Bismah rephrases 'the sun rises from the east'. Bismah is pleased with her daughter's progress but notes that she is only halfway through learning her alphabet.

Mydda has brought the rhyme book back and reads the second page of the poem. This time she is more confident, more fluent and needs fewer prompts.

> *Aadhi raat ko chaand – chaand* is the moon – *aur suraj* – I like that – *baadil kay koray (gharr) gharr aay (bijli) bijli ne durwa (za) durwaza kola dono he kha...* (Khab.) khab... (ra) khabra (ey) khabraey.
>
> *Suno gap shap, suno gap shap,*
>
> *nao me nali (nadi) nadi doob chali.*

Mydda continues to the end of the rhyme. Bismah reads the whole rhyme with expression, bringing out the rhythm of the piece. Mydda listens intently and gives a deep sigh. Spontaneously she starts explaining the text to me:

> That means, in the middle of the night, the moon came, and the sun, and the wind.
>
> Bismah: No, *baadil*, the clouds.
>
> Mydda: Clouds, in the middle of the night the moon and the sun went to *baadil*'s house.
>
> Bismah: Yes, cloud's house. And who opened the door? *Bijli*.

Mydda: *Bijli.*

Bismah: Lightning opened the door, so they were both frightened, or worried.

Although Mydda still needs help with decoding and a lot of vocabulary still presents a challenge, she loves the rhythm of the text and is determined to read it. Bismah is very pleased with her daughter's progress: 'This is the first time she has come so far. Now she says 'I want to read'.

The book of rhymes has rhythms and patterned language in Urdu that are difficult to reproduce in a translated text. Mydda is drawn to the music of the language and brings the book again on her next visit. This time she chooses to read *bander bandriya* (male monkey, female monkey) page 44. She needs a lot less prompting (in brackets).

> *Bandriya nay gagra pehna, Bandar ney shalwar, ban than kar jub ghar say niklay, ho gi takrar, bandriya ney ta (chari).* The story is different, it used to be *churi*, a knife, now it's a stick. *Bandriya ney chari batari (uthai) uthai , Bandar ney talwar, lartay lartay hoy (ho) ho gay (ghail) ghail kote (koi) koi na manay (mana) mana mer... her...(haar) haar.*

> (Female monkey wore the skirt, male monkey wore the trousers, they dressed up and came out of the house. They started arguing. Female monkey picked up the stick, male monkey picked up the sword. They got injured fighting. No one accepted defeat.)

As she finishes reading she stands up dramatically, asks her mother to sing the rhyme, joins in and performs the actions.

As Bismah commented, there is certainly a big difference in her confidence about recognising letters and decoding text. The primer is very structured and the rhymes are fun to learn. Mydda is proud and confident. I am curious to know whether her work with her grandmother over the summer and her continuing study with her mother will help her to read less well known text. I hope to find out at our next meeting.

Reading more advanced text

Bismah finds it hard to find time to read regularly with Mydda, but she has read her all the stories from *The Moving Mango Tree* (Jabeen, 1992). The stories are very similar to ones that she knows, although there are variations and they are told in a different style. The second story in the collection, *The Bad Crow,* is similar to the one she told me in Urdu when we first met, except she says that the characters are reversed.

The first story in the collection is about two cats and refers to the English character, Mother Hubbard. This is the story that Mydda wants to tell me about. She has the book on her lap, with the English text on the left and the Urdu on the right. There are no illustrations. She is keen to tell the story, but struggles and starts making it up.

'The two cats. Old Mother Hubbard ... I can't remember ... some food ... cat food.' Bismah laughs: 'They didn't have cat food in those days!' Mydda checks with the English text, which she can read fluently. But it doesn't help her to explain the Urdu, because the story is told slightly differently: the English text refers to feeding cats, the Urdu to feeding God's creatures.

Mydda continues and asks about *chapattis*. Bismah explains that she normally calls these *phulka*. 'There was monkeys and they ... chapattis as well... (Bismah prompts: 'did they try to steal them?'). I read it in English'. I ask her 'And Mummy read it in Urdu? Did you understand all the words in Urdu?' Mydda replies 'I understanded some!'

Bismah has mentioned before that, when reading to the children, she adapts the text to match their understanding. She suggests that she needs to read more often to Mydda in Urdu to develop her understanding of book language and extend her vocabulary. Although Mydda's attention span has improved, Bismah still finds her unwilling to sit still for long. 'She doesn't really like reading, although she is good at it. She prefers to draw and to write.'

In spite of the difficulties she experiences with understanding and her reported short attention span, Mydda is determined to show me that she can read the story herself, in Urdu. She starts decoding the very demanding text, with no illustrations for support. Bismah's prompts are in brackets.

Mydda, excitedly:

> *Do biliyan. Do biliyan.* (Two cats). *Mother Hubbard har jumerat ko za (Allah) Allah ki (mukhluk) mukhluk* (the creatures) *ko ko (kuch) kuch na koi (kuch) kuch dana (dayna) dayna basnad (pasand) basant karti thi. Es bar (usney) usney do bili (biliyoon) ko ek (chapatti) chapatti di. To (dono) dono biliay (biliyan) ko (jo)... (appus) appus mein na (bohot) bohot (ghehri) gheri (sehalian) sehalian (t.. in) thein (ch...p..) chapatti (pa) pa kar lar pa (parian) lar pari. Ek ney kama (kaha) kaha chapatti (yeh) yeh chapatti (meri) meri ha me (me hi) (sa ..r, sari) sari kahan (khaoun) khaoun gi...* (Jabeen, 1992:1)

Mydda decodes the page with great concentration. Bismah applauds. Mydda attempts again to explain the story to me in English:

'Mother Hubbard was making some chapattis for the two cats. And, I can't re-member what's her name, but someone came.' Bismah 'No! No one came! Don't think ahead, tell her this part of the story. It says she likes to give some food, every Thursday, to God's creatures.' Bismah discusses this with Mydda in Urdu. Mydda 'They were greedy, one ate it and there was none left for the other one'. Bismah:

> I don't think you understand. It says, they were great friends, but when they got the chapattis, they started fighting over it, because they were both hungry. And one said, it's mine, I will eat it and the other said no, how can this happen be-cause Mother Hubbard called me first. She gave it to me, and the first cat said, no, she likes me more than she likes you. That's the translation.

Mydda reads the English text:

> It was Thursday morning so old Mother Hubbard gave a small chapatti to her two cats, as she always liked to give them something extra on that day. The two cats who were friends began cruelly qua... (prompt from Bismah: quarelling) ... quarrelling (it means fighting, you know) over the bread. It's all mine, she gave it to me! Said one. No, I will have it, she called me first, the other said. She likes me. No, She prefers me to you, so the bread is mine!

Reading in English seems fairly transparent for Mydda, and she has few diffi-culties. However, reading in Urdu presents a double challenge. As well as the less familiar script, her use of Urdu is restricted to the family domain and stories are simplified in the telling to match her understanding. Words in her primer have been selected to be fairly easy to read for beginners, but this is not the case in the dual language texts. As was evident in her reading of *Brown Bear*, there are gaps in her vocabulary of even fairly common animal names and colours. So understanding the text and explaining it in English do not come easily to her. But her determination to decode complex text is remark-able. Mydda is treating the text as a code to be cracked, an exciting challenge that she is determined to meet.

Reading *Handa's surprise*

The *Moving Mango Tree* was perhaps a challenge too far. On the next visit she chooses a dual language picture book from the school's collection. While the text she has chosen, *Handa's Surprise* (Browne, 1994), is still a simple one for a reader of Mydda's experience in English, it has a clear story line and it is a book she enjoys.

She opens it confidently at page 3... and gets stuck right at the beginning. Bismah prompts her p... p.. t... *he* ... She recovers and decodes slowly but fluently: *pataa na nahen ous ko sub say acha phal kaun sa lagay ga.* (I wonder which fruit she'll like best?)

Mydda confidently tells me 'I work it out for myself', but then remembers the English wording and explains that it means 'I wonder what, which fruit she likes best.' She tells me that *phal* means fruit, that she remembers seeing the word in her alphabet book, and she looks it up to show me. On the next page, she points out the word *kaila* to me and explains that it means banana.

Many teachers have used this text to promote discussion about fruit. As well as showing that she now remembers key vocabulary, Mydda engages in a discussion with her mother about guavas. Bismah explains that she knows the fruit in English, but not its Urdu name: 'Do you remember guava? You can buy them here, in special shops'.

Mydda reads the text on page 6 in both languages, with a few prompts in Urdu: '*Kia wo russi (rus) rus bhar (bhara) rus bhara sankatra (sangtra) sangtra basand karay gi* (Will she like the round juicy orange) and this prompts a discussion about oranges available in England and Pakistan. Mydda has identified *sungtra* as orange. Bismah explains that usually orange is *malta*.

> I don't think you have *sungtra* here. It's like, not a clementine, almost pear-shaped. It's very sour, not sweet. My mother used to like them. They are oranges, but they peel off very easily, and they are pear-shaped. The fruit inside is not pear-shaped, but the peel is pear-shaped. It's small and it's very, very sour. I like *mossammis*. You don't have them here either. The peel is orange, they are white inside and creamy and they're very sweet. They are never sour. *Narangi* is also orange.

Later in the text when Mydda has explained to me that *ananas* means pineapple, Bismah informs me the word originates from Arabic.

Mydda wants to move on and launches rapidly into reading the rest of the book: showing off her decoding skills is what she really wants to do, even though she has already been working on demanding text for 45 minutes. When she comes to the end of the book, she remembers having seen an ostrich in her Urdu alphabet book and goes looking for the Urdu word.

Bismah explains that from being a reluctant reader, not managing to remember her letters from one reading session with her mother to the next, Mydda has now overtaken her older brother in her decoding skills and is very proud of herself.

Discussion

The school's commitment to involving parents and community is much in evidence and Bismah has frequently told stories in Urdu and worked alongside teachers to encourage children's use of Urdu. The complexity of children's language and literacy backgrounds is understood and this is helpful for Mydda, whose relationship with Urdu within the family is complex. There is little to show her hybrid identity: she wears a tracksuit to school and speaks like the born east Londoner that she is. The complex reality of her language use is revealed in her diagram. The opportunity to use dual language books with her mother, supported by the family visit, reinforced her Pakistani heritage. As well as providing opportunities to speak Urdu with her cousins, the visit left a lasting legacy by offering the key to the complexities of the Urdu script. Her enthusiasm for this aspect of her heritage is evident in her love of Urdu rhymes and stories and her pleasure in discussing the pictures in the primer and hearing about the oranges that grow in Pakistan.

In their reading together, Bismah has deployed a range of strategies to support Mydda at all levels: she draws attention to sounds in words, suggests she blend them to make words as she does in English, prompts her discreetly to support the flow of her reading, gives advice on pronunciation and explains vocabulary across English and Pakistani culture. She interprets both text and culture for her daughter and models reading in a way that makes Mydda sigh with pleasure and envy. While she may sound strict in the transcript when she corrects Mydda's errors, there is a smile in her voice and much patience.

Mydda is creative in her response to Urdu texts and uses both the skills and knowledge she has developed to read in English with the strategies suggested by her grandmother's primer. When reading *Brown Bear* or *Handa's Surprise* she makes full use of her knowledge of the conventions of this kind of text, the patterned language, the repetition, the illustrations. The use of the Urdu primer with its focus on the bottom-up strategy of sound/symbol identification and the learning of alliterative rhymes, allied to her knowledge of how she learned to blend sounds in English, eventually provided the key that enabled her to attempt the complex text of the Two Cats story.

The ability to make hypotheses based on the overall meaning of the text to predict is a valuable top-down skill that can assist fluency and speed in reading. Mydda's hypothesis-making is hampered by her shortage of vocabulary in Urdu and is less successful. Bismah noted that she would find learning to read much easier if her knowledge of spoken Urdu were greater. Like the children described in Gregory, Long and Volk (2004) she is bringing together strategies learned from one language to the other, checking words found in a dual text book with her Urdu primer. But it is the challenge of cracking the secret of the Urdu letter/sound correspondence that focuses most of her attention. Her reported short attention span is nowhere in evidence as she tackles page after page and is intent on showing that she can decode unknown text.

Mydda's understanding of what she reads is still uncertain and her use of metalinguistic strategies is limited. Meaning in English is totally clear, meaning in Urdu a little cloudy and she sometimes struggles to make connections across her languages, making less use than other children in the study of the two languages on the page. Her experience is a reminder that not all bilingual children take readily to translating between their languages.

There is an interesting example in the following transcript in which Mydda, guided by Bismah, explains a phrase in her primer:

> *Tefil baag mein kheltay hein.* This one is kids (*tefil*) and park, different kids, park
>
> Bismah asks Mydda to translate. She is puzzled 'Do you mean read it?'
>
> Bismah: What does it mean in English, tell me in English?
>
> Mydda: Kids ... park ...
>
> Bismah: No, no don't translate word by word, make a sentence.
>
> Mydda: Kids play in the park.

The strongest development that emerges over the few months that the observed sessions have taken place is the transformation of Mydda's identity as a learner. 'She can read, but she doesn't like it,' reported her mother, of her reading in English. 'She has an attention span of about ten minutes, she learns some Urdu, then, as often as not, forgets it all by the next session.' In the course of learning to read Urdu with her mother, Mydda's curiosity, persistence and determination have turned her into an enthusiastic and committed reader .

7

Practice, pleasure and persistence
Collaborative learning in Turkish

Those who are good at something... achieve mastery by practice, pleasure and persistence' wrote Margaret Meek in a booklet that has inspired a whole generation of teachers to use good literature to teach children to read (1988:3). Lek and Durkan are not yet considered good at reading and they are still a little short on practice, but their scores on pleasure, persistence, and pride as well, are very high.

I was invited to meet six children who had encountered dual language books in English and Turkish in the course of sessions designed to support their reading in English. They asked their teacher if they could help each other to read in Turkish. When I first met the children (five boys and one girl) they were lively, boisterous and excited about sharing their knowledge of reading in Turkish. All sounded, in English, like typical London school children. They were eager to talk about how they used their languages at home and to demonstrate to me what they knew about reading in Turkish. Their parents were intent on keeping the language alive: Durkan explained that his father insisted on Turkish at home. Their teacher had responded to their enthusiasm by encouraging them to help each other and also to borrow the dual language books to read with their parents.

My observations of the children were very different from the ones reported in the earlier chapters of this book. Their parents all agreed to their children's involvement in the research, but I did not get to meet them. I focused initially on Lek and Nilhan, two keen readers, who had both learned some very basic reading at Turkish school, and was able to observe how they used a range of strategies and their complementary skills to support each other. The following tells the story of my second observational visit to the school.

Collaborative learning

On this occasion I find that Nilhan has moved to another school and that Lek and Durkan are eagerly awaiting me. They explain that they are best friends and want to read with me together. As they check through the school's collection of dual language books, Durkan spots *The Giant Turnip* (Barkow, 2001a) and his eyes light up 'I read that! It gets bigger!' Durkan tells me he can read 'a little bit' in Turkish. The boys agree that they will take turns at reading, but that they will help each other out as necessary.

The session was intended to last twenty minutes as their teacher knew they were both likely to find the reading demanding. They were bubbling with excitement and so highly motivated that, in the event, they read for well over an hour.

As a researcher I had strong reservations about working with the children in a language I don't know, unaccompanied by a speaker of Turkish. As I studied the recording after the session I realised that, in this particular instance, my being a non-Turkish speaker was a bonus. The children did not see me as a teacher. I wasn't going to tell them whether they got it right or wrong. They knew Turkish, they were the experts and they were going to explain things to me. In the same way as the young bilingual children in Kenner's study (2004) revealed their understanding of their two languages by teaching them to other children, so Lek and Durkan revealed theirs to me as they worked together to understand the text and answer my questions.

The collaboration between two friends revealed the many different ways in which the children were making meaning from the text, negotiating with each other in two languages, using all their decoding skills, background knowledge and any clues they could get from the book as well as their knowledge of traditional tales to understand the story. The long session, during which the children read the whole book, enabled me to focus closely on the strategies they were using.

Reading the words – in Turkish

Lek starts to read first and Durkan whispers support (in brackets).

> Lek reads: *Kocaman ... Sal...* (Durkan: *Şalgam*)... *Şal...gam.* Durkan corrects Lek's pronunciation from *salgam* to *Şalgam* (pronounced *shalgam*. The title of the book: *The Giant Turnip*).

> Lek reads: *Bayeram* (Durkan corrects: *bayan*) *bayan Honeywood'un sınıfında oku... oku* (Durkan: *okuyan*) *çocuklar her yıl okulum bahçesinde sebze ve meyva yetis...* (Durkan: *yetiştirirler*)...

100

Lek and Durkan together: *yetiştirirler.*

(Every year the children in Miss Honeywood's class grow some fruit and vegetables in the school garden) (Barkow, 2001:1)

Like Lek, Durkan has attended Turkish classes some time ago. He appears to have a more confident grasp of grapho-phonic correspondence in Turkish than Lek. From the evidence of this and similar extracts Durkan is able both to supply words that Lek is struggling to read (such as *okuyan* and *yetiştirirler*) and to correct his pronunciation (of *Şalgam,* for example). He intervenes in a similar way on page 5. When Lek reads: *Yazda çocuklar bitki...bitki* (Durkan corrects: *bitkileri*) *bitkileri besleyip suladılar. Ve tüm yaban otları söktüler* (In the summer the children fed and watered the plants. And pulled out all the weeds), Durkan corrects his pronunciation of *suladılar* and reads the last two words of the text alongside him.

In the following examples it is Lek who helps Durkan to read the word topraği (the soil).

Durkan reads: *Ikbaharnn başlarında, şocuklar topra.. topra* (Lek offers: *topraği*) *topraği, kazarak ve tırmıklayarak hazırladılar* (In early spring the children prepared the ground by digging and raking the soil.) (p3)

The children, and Lek in particularly, read very carefully, confident with some words, painstakingly decoding others, but as they progress through the book their confidence and speed of reading increases. They alternate and a pattern emerges: whoever chips in to support, continues so that the extract often ends with both children reading together. Sometimes the combined efforts of both children are needed to work out a long word, such as *atlattıkan* (p8). It is clear that both children know their Turkish phonics well and they are proud of their skill.

Reading the words – in English

The children take turns to read the pages and whoever starts in Turkish also reads the English. Lek reads fluently with no miscues. Durkan's reading is hesitant but correct, except on page 3 where he reads: 'In early Spring, the children pre.. prepared the ground by digging and rakking the soil'. He works out 'prepared' for himself but his pronunciation of 'raking' suggests he is not familiar with the word and Lek corrects him. Later, on page 5, he misreads another word, also suggesting unfamiliarity with the meaning and, again, Lek corrects him. He reads 'When Miss Honeywood has recorded (Lek corrects: recovered) recovered from the shock, she asked how are we going to get the turnip out?'

From the evidence of this session both children have good phonic knowledge and can decode text confidently in English at the level of the picture books used.

The meaning of words

As a non-Turkish speaker I can never be sure, when a child cannot explain a word in English, whether the issue is a lack of knowledge in Turkish or in English. The transcript of Lek and Durkan reading together reveals some interesting strategies for dealing with words they find difficult to explain in English.

When Durkan is speaking in English, there are numerous instances where he uses the word 'thing' – as in the following extract.

> *Bir iple bağlıp hep birlikte çekebiliriz, diye önerdi Samira. Bu çok iyi bir fikir, dedi Bayan Honeywood. Lee ve Michael siz gidip uzun, gidip ozun, ipi getirin* (We could tie a rope around it and all pull together, suggested Samira. That's a good idea, said Mrs Honeywood, Lee and Michael, go and get the long rope.) (p12)

He has read the Turkish text and is using the illustration and both texts to explain to me in English:

> 'He gets a rope ... and then the ... first he says *thing*, let's get a rope and then the teacher says 'nice thinking' and then *thing*, they get the rope ... Lee and Michael ... they get the *thing*, a good rope.'

"Bir iple bağlayıp hep birlikte çekebiliriz," diye önerdi Samira.
"Bu çok iyi bir fikir," dedi Bayan Honeywood. "Lee ve Michael, siz gidip uzun ipi getirin."

"We could tie a rope around it and all pull together," suggested Samira.
"That's a good idea," said Miss Honeywood. "Lee and Michael, you go and get the long rope."

The Giant Turnip (Barkow, 2001a: 11-12)

The illustration represents two children carrying a rope from the school building towards the enormous turnip which is partly visible. Durkan starts to describe the picture. He is struggling to tell me in English what the first sentence of dialogue means (*Bir iple bağlayıp hep birlikte çekebiliriz* – we could tie a rope around it and pull it together) and summarises it as 'thing'. He is then able to translate correctly for me ('nice thinking') the comment made by the teacher (in the text *Bu çok iyi bir fakir*, that's a good idea). He uses 'thing' again twice in the sentence, not so much to replace a word or phrase, because he clearly knows the word 'rope' which occurs twice in the English text, but seemingly to provide thinking time.

There are several other examples of this use of 'thing'. Durkan uses the same tactic when explaining what is happening on page 14. The Turkish text is *Biz erkeklerden daha güclüyüz* (we're stronger than the boys), which Durkan explains as 'They're saying, they're saying like *thing*, we'll be better than the boys'.

There are other instances where 'thing' seems to be filling in a vocabulary lack, for example when Durkan is describing a picture that shows weeds in a wheelbarrow (p5): 'the weeds inside the *thing*'.

Lek is generally more confident in speaking in English and there is only one instance in this transcript of him using 'thing'. On page 4 the Turkish text reads:

> *Daha sonra, yine ilkbaharda, kirağı tehlikesi geçtikten sonra tohumları ektiler* (Later in the spring, when there was no danger of frost, they planted the seeds). He uses it in very much the same way as Durkan, both to gain time and to fill in a gap: 'it's about *thing*, they're putting these *things*.'

When it comes to assessing difficulties with Turkish it is essential for a Turkish speaker to be able to question the children and evaluate responses and retellings. As noted before, when they have read the Turkish text and been asked to explain it in English, both children have a tendency either to describe the picture or tell what they know of the story. In many instances the explanations make fairly minimal reference to the Turkish text, but it is not easy to determine whether this is because of a lack of understanding of the Turkish or a difficulty in expressing the meaning in English. Translation is a sophisticated skill that does not necessarily come easily to children who have little occasion to practise it. The data above suggests that the use of 'thing' could well be a tactic to gain thinking time.

Durkan seems more fluent in Turkish and is more confident at decoding text. However the following example suggests that his difficulties in understanding and expressing himself may not be restricted to English. After reading:

> *Çocuklar yaz tatillerinden döndüklerinde sebze ve meyvaların büyüdüğünü gördüler* (when the children came back, after their summer holiday, they found that all the fruit and vegetables had grown). (p6)

Durkan tries to explain the meaning and then admits 'I don't really know'.

Lek seems more fluent in English but may have greater difficulty in understanding the Turkish. When asked, after reading a passage in Turkish, to explain its meaning, his most common approach is to launch into a very fluent account of the story as he knows it, rather than to explain or paraphrase the meaning of the Turkish or indeed the English text.

'Connectives and stuff': understanding the structure of words and sentences

Where my status as a non-speaker of Turkish is a bonus is when the children, working together to understand the structure of the languages they know, take on the role of teacher to explain to me how Turkish works and how they make sense of the text in two languages. As they explore the structure of words in Turkish and word order within the sentence, Lek takes the lead. The following discussion shows Lek and Durkan exploring the morphology of two key words in the Turkish text. They have just read page 7 together:

> *Ama şalgamı görünce gözlerine inanamadılar! Bir zürafadan daha uzun ve bir filden daha genişti* (But when they saw the turnip, they could hardly believe their eyes! It was taller than a giraffe, and wider than an elephant.)

In answer to a question, both children respond together and try to explain the significance of the suffix *-den* (*bir filden daha*: – er than an elephant, in this case 'wider'). They tell me that 'elephant' is *fil*, or is it *filden*? They argue: '*fil* is not, *filden* is not, I think … *fil* is an elephant'. Lek explores the word: '*fil* is an elephant, but *filden* is like, it can be flower or another big elephant, or another big one.' Durkan agrees that *filden* means bigger. Lek muses: '*filde*, smaller, but *filde*, you add *-en* and it gets bigger'.

Once again Durkan agrees and then he tells me that *zürafada* means giraffe. Lek picks up on this and considers how this relates to his explanations about the *fil* and *filden*: 'you add *-an* and it makes it bigger. If you spell *zürafada*, that's just a giraffe, but if you add *-an*, it makes it like, more popular, it's like there's more giraffes'. Durkan intervenes to suggest that this addition means bigger and Lek expands: 'if you have, like, connectives and stuff, it makes the word bigger'.

Turkish is an agglutinative language and its morphological structure is very different from English. Lek has not made any direct comparisons between the two, but he has connected the grammar he has learned in English lessons in school with his understanding of the meaning of the suffixes on *fild-en* and *zürafa-dan*. Durkan comments on the fact that Turkish can have some very long words. Lek's explanation of this suggests that, although he is struggling to express it, he understands that Turkish words have a core and that the suffixes establish the precise meaning of the word in the context of the sentence. Both children have an awareness of this but have an, as yet, limited understanding of the exact meaning of the various suffixes: Lek's reference to *zürafada* (on the giraffe) is not relevant to the meaning in this context. Lek explains: 'Because, like, because it's not, they're not big, 'cos some people just add, like ... connectives to it, to make it, like, more interesting. Then it makes it better.' In this instance, he seems to be referring to his literacy lessons in English in which he would have been introduced to technical vocabulary like connectives.

In the following extract, Lek takes on the role of teacher and explains the passage to me using a word-for-word translation. The Turkish text on page 9 reads:

> *Ben biliyorum, dedi Kieran, bir helikopterle çekerek çıkartabiliriz* ('I know, we could get a helicopter to pull it out,' said Kieran').

Lek explains:

> 'That means I (pointing to *ben*) and that means *biliyorum*, that know, and *dedi* is words and *Kieran* is like, a name for Kieran, and *helikopter* is helicopter and *çekerek* I think it is could and this one is (the last word, *çıkartabiliriz*) is pulled'.

Although he does not explicitly comment on the differences in word order, Lek is carefully looking for ways of matching the Turkish and English texts. While he has expressed his agreement with Lek, Durkan has not directly contributed to this analysis or commented on word order.

Understanding the whole text
Although he has carried out some close analyses of the text, Lek prefers to use a range of clues as well as his understanding of key words in the text. Both children use, in varying degrees, the English text, the illustrations and their own wider knowledge of the conventions of picture books as well as the tradi-

tional story of *The Enormous Turnip*. Sometimes, in my role as the person who does not understand Turkish, I ask the children if they would explain to me a passage they have just read. This triggers complex discussions and a use of many different strategies.

As the children read '*Bayan Honeywood un sınıfında okuyan çocuklar her yil okulum bahçesinde sebze ve meyva yetiştirirler*' (p1) they struggle with the last word. Lek suggests that it means 'catch up' and Durkan agrees (they are almost correct, but, in this context, it actually means 'to grow').

I probably look sceptical, as this word does not seem to match the English translation, and Lek offers 'It says every year the children they, in Miss Honeywood, in her class, every day they pick fruit and vegetables in the school garden'. Durkan again agrees and Lek refers to the English text and reads 'Every year the children in Miss Honeywood's class grow some fruit and vegetables in the school garden'. However, neither child comments on the difference between the English text and the translation offered by Lek. The latter suggests that he has understood most of the sentence and probably used his knowledge of the story. However his interpretation implies that he has misunderstood the verb, that long difficult word at the end of the sentence, which means 'grow' but which Lek has translated first as 'catch up' and then as 'pick'. I am interested that he has been content with his approximate translation and not used the English text to refer back to the meaning of the Turkish.

Clues on the page: the two texts and the pictures
In the extract above, the English explanation of the Turkish text offered by the children was very close to the English translation, although the latter was not used to check for accuracy.

Lek makes greater use of both texts (as well as the illustration) in his reading of page 5. After reading the Turkish text '*Yazda çocuklar bitkileri beslieyip suladilar. Ve tüm yaban otları söktüler*' he explains that it means 'In this the spring the children fed and watered the plants and they pulled the weeds, the roots out, they pulled the roots out ... the weeds inside the thing'. In this interpretation he uses part of a sentence from the English text which reads 'in the summer the children fed and watered the plants. And pulled out all the weeds', and refers to it to correct his original suggestion that the children were pulling out the roots, although he fails to notice that the English version refers to summer. The last phrase in his explanation comes from his interpretation of the illustration which shows weeds in a wheelbarrow.

Lek makes little further use of the parallel texts until page 16. Durkan reads the Turkish: '*Ama şalgam yine, şalgam yine kımıldamadı*' (But the turnip still would not move) and both children struggle to read the last word. Durkan works it out and exclaims triumphantly 'It never moved!' Lek tries to explain the problem by using the illustration, but seems to have some trouble interpreting it: 'I think it's stuck under the... this... this... grey thing'. He agrees when I suggest that the grey thing is the ground. He rolls the word *kımıldamadı* around in his mouth and reflects 'but the turnip still didn't, never moved', then checks the English and reads with satisfaction 'but the turnip still would not move'.

Durkan does not find it easy to explain to me in English what he has just read in Turkish and rarely refers to the English text for support, except in the two following examples. He reads the text on page 6 with enthusiasm and confidence and just a little help from Lek with the last two words.

> '*Çocuklar yaz tatillerinden döndüklerinde... döndüklerinde, sebze ve meyvaların büyü... büyüdü .. büyüdüğünü gördüler*' (When the children came back, after their summer holiday, they found all the fruit and vegetables had grown).

In response to my usual question, Durkan tries to explain 'The children ... I think it was called the hot...'

Lek intervenes: 'It's not hot, it's, like, the season.' I ask if he means 'summer' and Durkan agrees 'summer, yeah.' I ask again 'what do you think it's saying?' Durkan reflects for a while 'I don't really know'.

I suggest he looks at the English text and he starts reading 'When the children came back after their summer ...' He leaps with excitement 'Yeah! It was their holiday' and reads on confidently.

Durkan read the Turkish on page 10 with some help from Lek: *Veya bir vinçle onu kaldıra kaldırabiliriz diye önerdi Ta... Ta...* (Lek: 'He said that wrong') *önerdi* (Lek: Yeah, that's it') *Tarik* (Or we could get a crane to lift it, suggested Tariq). In the following conversation Lek and Durkan are trying to make sense of the sentence. Lek suggests '*Tarak* (comb) is something like you do your hair' and Durkan offers an alternative, cued by the illustration of a mechanical digger: '*Tarak* is something like there's a machine and it goes (makes tapping noise on the table) ... like that'. After a discussion about the meaning of *kaldırabiliriz* which Lek works out means 'to pick up' Durkan solves the Tarik mystery by referring to the English text 'I think he's called Tarik'.

However, later in the book, where the English text reads:

and it wobbled this way and that and then it slowly moved. They pulled even harder and at last the turnip rolled out of its hole and onto the grass. The class cheered and danced around with joy.

Durkan, by reading the Turkish and using clues from the picture, has made sense of the text and paraphrases it: 'When the turnip came up they started dancing. They, it says, they pulled it more harder'.

Clues beyond the page – knowledge of stories

Knowledge of the nature of a text and the cultural features that locate it in a tradition provide powerful supports for reading and interpreting, since they enable the reader to make predictions (Meek, 1988). Young children learning to read through well loved folk tales and popular picture books use their knowledge of the text and the cues from the illustrations to support their developing skills. So much so that many children learn favourite texts by heart and can lead a casual listener to think they are fluent readers. Evidence from the transcript suggests that the children's knowledge of the traditional story of the enormous turnip sometimes gets in the way of their interpreting the actual text on the page. This is most noticeable with Lek.

The illustrations and the names of children who feature in the story (Samira, Tarik, Kate) indicate that the version told here has transposed the tale to the garden of a school in an ethnically mixed part of Britain. In passing, it provides lessons on how to plant seeds and care for vegetables. The strategies involved in pulling the turnip out of the ground reflect an urban, technologically sophisticated society, as opposed to the old-fashioned, rural society that is the usual context for this folk tale. But the basic structure of the tale is the same.

Early on in the book, while looking at page 3 where the illustration shows children preparing the ground (and there is no sign or mention of a turnip), Lek and Durkan get very excited and both talk at the same time to tell me what is going to happen. Lek exclaims 'And that big thing! It's going to grow, the turnip!' and Durkan cuts in with 'And the people can't get out, and there's lots of people trying to pull it out, and when it pulled, they say 'hurray!' then they eat, I think'.

Later in the story, in the part of the text that tells of the turnip becoming wider than an elephant, Lek reads the Turkish but, rather than explain the meaning to me, he is inspired by a picture of the turnip that fills the entire page and struggles to explain in greater detail:

> When the turnip got bigger, the people didn't know that they put too much weed inside it, and it got bigger and bigger and nobody couldn't pulled it, that's why, that's why the people came and needs a lot of help to pull it and, who pulled it, when everybody pulled it, all those people pulled it and it... it, all that hard work and people pulled it, they get to eat the turnip.

Later still Lek and Durkan argue about how the story will end. Lek suggests 'I think it will finish when they pull it out' but Durkan disagrees 'No! I think they eat it!'

While Durkan attempts to paraphrase and predict, it is clear that Lek loves the opportunity to move into story telling mode. After reading page 5 which shows the turnip seed being planted and watered, and weeds pulled out, Durkan predicts 'I bet they forgot one and then the thing going to get bigger!' But Lek launches into his own personalised narrative:

> Once I went to this place in the garden and there was a big, there was a big turnip, and we couldn't get it out and, at the bottom there was roots, and at the bottom there was a hole, so somebody got under. Me and, me and my cousin and my other cousin and we was trying to get the turnip out, and somebody has to go under and take the root out. And I done it and I, when I went under, I saw the root, I just pushed it, then my cousin and my other cousin got the spades and the, and pushed it a little bit and then I just punched and the turnip came out.

Whenever I ask the children about the meaning of bits of the story, what I get in response is often neither a translation nor a paraphrase of the text, but a much fuller account that draws from all the resources the children have found in the text and from their knowledge of the cultural context.

Discussion

I had opportunities to observe several of the children reading over a period of a few months, but the session with Lek and Durkan has been chosen for this chapter because they were representative of the group and the session encapsulated most of the features observed. The snapshot of the session was revealing for me, in my role as observer of children as experts and collaborative learners.

Texts that teach

The work of Meek has demonstrated how good quality children's picture books actively support inexperienced readers. Lek and Durkan use the illustrations, predict from their knowledge of traditional tales and are supported by appropriate language structures. The culture of shared classroom texts also supports the readers. Lek and Durkan have a knowledge and love of the traditional stories that they have encountered in their classroom and this propels them on to make hypotheses about what will happen and look for further textual clues. While the children have generally sound strategies for decoding words in both languages, their still imperfect knowledge of the two languages means they are still much in need of the support offered by an interesting, relevant and well structured text.

The additional clue in the texts provided by a second language turns the whole reading task into a complex linguistic and cultural puzzle which the children find challenging but enjoyable. As they compare and contrast, the process begins to lead them into an understanding of the ways in which their two languages differ. Of all the children in this study, they are the ones who comment most on this.

Culture and identity

The use of translated stories breaks down barriers between cultures (Meek, 2001) as it introduces children to many different story traditions. These help teachers to create a multicultural space in their classroom where children can recognise themselves in the teaching resources used. They provide the safe space that Creese *et al* (2006) describe in their study of complementary schools in which children can explore and develop a multicultural identity as they find opportunities for discussion and the sharing of experience. However, the strong bias in commercially published dual language books towards the western European folk tale tradition can make it difficult to find texts that reflect the cultures of all the children. The books the children chose to read to me did not reflect Turkish culture and their attraction for the children was the availability of the Turkish text.

Creese *et al* have referred to children developing their identity as learners. The children in this part of the study had been identified as 'not good readers'. The way in which they struggled in varying degrees with the texts is much in evidence in the transcripts. In the encounters I had with the Turkish children, what was striking was the way in which they were redefining themselves. From admitting to not being good readers, especially in Turkish (Lek: 'I'm not really good at reading Turkish'), by the time Lek and Durkan met with me for the long session with The Giant Turnip book, they were operating in quite a different mode: they were cracking a puzzle, they were highly motivated; they were punching the air and shouting 'Yeah!' when they understood something that challenged them. However daunting the task, they were working on it together, succeeding most of the time in cracking the code, and learning was becoming fun. Their current teacher had given them an opportunity to read in Turkish and my presence and interest turned them into experts. The strength of their commitment was evident in the session recorded above in their wish to go on reading long after they should have returned to their class.

Meek tells us how children draw on the whole of their culture when reading and writing 'if we let them' (1988:38). While behaving and sounding exactly like the London-born children that they are, there is evidence in the following extract that the children are drawing on the whole of their culture. Lek and Durkan read together:

> *Ayçiçeği, bezelye, ve şalgam yetiştirmeğe ...* (they struggle with this)
>
> Durkan: *karar verdiler.*
>
> (They decided to grow sunflowers, peas and turnips.)

The reference to the turnip reminds the children of a Turkish drink which they describe to me:

> RS: So what does that mean then?
>
> Lek: It's a turnip and sometimes Turkish people turn the turnip, they do something with another fruit, I don't know and they just put it together and they squeeze it and...
>
> Durkan: A drink.
>
> RS: You make a drink with it?
>
> Durkan: And they put, children can drink it but, it's a little bit hot, it's a little bit...
>
> RS: Is it strong?.
>
> Durkan: No, it's a little bit like...
>
> Lek: It's a little bit thing, like, it's bad.
>
> RS: Is it bitter?
>
> Durkan: No, it's hot.
>
> RS: Spicy?
>
> Lek: Spicy.
>
> RS: Spicy hot.
>
> Durkan: Oh, I know and it's red.
>
> Lek: They get, they put it in the machine, like four turnips and they squeeze and it, it turns, it goes in a special machine, so they can take the germs and things out, and sometimes they clean it and put in a factory and then they take it to shops, then people get buy it.

Durkan: Sometimes it ain't hot.

Lek: Sometimes it's sweet, for children. But the hot ones are for ... Yes, I did, the hot one, I drank. It's so hot!

I later find out that the children are referring to *Şalgam suy,* a spicy drink made from pickled turnip juice.

As the dinner hour approaches, Lek starts to tell me about the Turkish books he has at home and sometimes reads with his mother. Durkan explains that he doesn't have many books but sometimes reads with Lek when he goes to his house. But there is competition there from a playstation game in Turkish, featuring a scenario played out in Istanbul.

The children then proceed to tell me how I could learn Turkish. Lek suggests:

First you would have to, like, go to Turkey and you have, like, listen to people and like, learn the words. You go to Turkey and if they know English they'll tell you the Turkish. And then, they'll say it in English what it is. Or you could go to Turkish school and learn. To adult school. Or you can just listen to people so you can learn Turkish.

And Durkan adds 'And you could get a bodyguard to tell you everything'.

Suddenly Lek boasts of all the rhymes that his grandmother knows. 'My Granma, my Grandmother teached me that and she knows 108 of them. At Turkey everybody knows different songs with hands. I just know 10.' He jumps up. Durkan hesitates, he's not sure he knows them. Lek demonstrates and the session ends in a very lively performance of several intricate hand clapping songs.

8

Sarah the reader

J'ai appris à lire en Français d'abord. J'ai appris toute seule parce qu'ils me montraient seulement des mots et puis j'avais acheté des petits livres que mes cousins avaient envoyés de Belgique.

(I learned to read in French first. I taught myself because they showed me words and then I bought little books that my cousins sent me from Belgium)

Thirty eight different languages are spoken in Sarah's east London Primary school. The school was participating in the Developing Literacy through Home Languages Project. When I was invited to visit the school to meet Lek and Durkan and their group of Turkish speaking children, I also met Sarah. Sarah spoke my language and was teaching herself and so my role in this case study was quite different: instead of being an observer I became an active participant.

Sarah and language

Sarah is 9 years old. She was born in London to parents recently arrived from the Democratic Republic of Congo (DRC) where French is the language of education. She has an older sister and a twin brother and cousins in France and Belgium whom she occasionally visits.

Sarah has a quiet manner but is very confident about language and passionate about reading. She speaks fluent English and French and understands Lingala, a language of the DRC. She explains that her parents speak French and Lingala between themselves, and Lingala when they meet with family in Belgium. She reports that she generally speaks French with her family and English, at her mother's request, when visitors are present. Sarah has never met her grandmother who lives in the Congo, but she speaks to her on the telephone and writes to her in French. Sarah's first language was

French and she reports learning English when she started school at the age of 5. She does not remember having a problem with understanding what was going on around her and she declares proudly '*j'ai parlé tout de suite*' (I spoke straight away) which suggests that she may have picked up English from her environment before starting school.

She tells me her strongest language is now English, but she mostly chooses to speak to me in French.

She explains that she taught herself to read when she was 4, with a little help from her mother and older sister. She remembers little about learning to read in English, except that it seems to have been completely painless:

> the teachers read a lot of stories to us. Then there was some work, dot-to-dot and you followed the letters. And then we got to make our own stories... I wrote loads of stories.

Sarah loves writing stories, but this is always in English. Her teacher confirms her story and recalls that she has been able to decode print accurately since Reception class.

Sarah explains that her parents do not know where to buy children's books in French. She was therefore very excited when the EMA teacher in her school offered her the opportunity to borrow dual language books in French and English. She has now read the school's entire stock of 22 books, some of them several times over.

Sarah reading dual language books

In the course of my first two visits, Sarah reads to me fluently and with expression in both languages from a selection of dual language picture books. Her skills in both languages seem evenly matched, although she occasionally mispronounces French verbs in the past tense: *craignant* for *craignaient, faisant for faisait.*

It is clear from her reading that she understands the texts. As she prefers to read the French text first, I fish a little to check her understanding of words that may be less familiar. As she reads from *Not Again Red Riding Hood* (Clynes and Daykin, 2003) '*Le Petit Chaperon Rouge jouait dans le jardin après sa terrible épreuve avec le méchant loup*' (Red Riding Hood was playing in the garden after her terrible ordeal with that nasty wolf, p1), I ask her what *épreuve* means. She explains by translating it into the English word 'experience'. When I suggest the word might mean something more disagreeable, she reads the English text but finds that the word 'ordeal' is also unfamiliar. She re-reads the text and figures out that it is means an unpleasant experience.

As she reads other texts I realise that, like many children who have taught themselves to read, Sarah has strong top-down strategies and makes full use of context when encountering unfamiliar words. She has an extensive vocabulary in both languages and it is noticeable, from several similar instances, that when a word is unfamiliar in one language, it is often unfamiliar in the other, so that the translated text does not support her. The word *banquet* encountered in *Beowulf* (Barkow, 2002) is exactly the same in both languages. Relying on the context, she suggests *fête*. In the same text both *ménestrel* and minstrel are unfamiliar and she suggests '*des ménestrels c'est des gens qui jouent de la guitare et tout*' (minstrels are people who play the guitar and stuff). The inferences she makes always make sense in the context and I wonder whether her good hypothesising skills are supported by having two different but parallel contexts.

Later in the Beowulf story, the English text does help her when I ask the meaning of *emporter* in the context *Grendel va venir vous emporter* (Grendel will come and drag you away). Initially she explains it means '*il va venir pour te tuer*' which makes sense in the context of the story, but is not the correct meaning. She then suggests '*Il va te prendre. Il va te mettre dans un autre pays*' (he will come and take you. He will put you in another country) which also makes sense in the context. We then discuss what I might be going to do if I said I was going to *emporter* the book on the table, and she suggests 'borrow'. Only then does Sarah look at the English version of the text and she laughs when she reads 'come and drag you away'.

When asked to read a completely unfamiliar text from a teacher's home-made selection of stories, she reads faultlessly until she encounters numbers in the written text. I am very surprised to find that she cannot read numbers above single digits and that she thinks the word *cent* (one hundred) means seven.

Sarah reading advanced texts
Wanting to pursue the investigation of Sarah's reading with parallel texts and being unable to locate more dual language books that would present a challenge to her, I went looking for children's literature in French that was also available in English translation. I drew a blank in London bookshops. The French children's sections were awash with French translations of English texts. Of the available texts at the appropriate level I chose *Harry Potter and the Philosopher's Stone* (Rowling, 1997) in French and matched it to the

original English from my own bookshelves. I also chose *Les quatre filles du Dr March, Little Women* (Alcott, 1994) which I remembered from my own childhood as being a high quality French translation.

The books are side by side, matched page for page. Sarah chooses to read the Harry Potter first and this time she starts to read in English first. She reads fluently, with expression and virtually faultlessly, running her finger rapidly along the line of print. She briefly gives me the gist of what she has read:

> It's about this family, they like to show off a bit, like, the Mum is, like, spying on the neighbours and the Dad thinks he's big and strong. They don't like, the lady doesn't like her sister. Because she says they're not part of the family.

When asked why she thinks that, she suggests 'Because they're unusual people'.

Sarah told me that English was now her stronger language. I saw little evidence of this when she read the dual language picture books and she seemed to have broadly equal skills in both languages. When she starts reading the Harry Potter text in French however, she reads more slowly and hesitates slightly over a few words. There are a number of miscues in her reading and they are of an interesting nature. She is reading for meaning and the miscues she makes indicate that she is predicting the text and reading what she expects.

For example, for *mais toutes deux ne s'étaient plus revues* (but neither had seen the other again), she reads *mais toutes deux ne s'étaient pas... plus revues*, adding the *pas* that she would most commonly expect to find after *ne* as a negative in conversation. In the same vein, in place of *Mrs Dursley faisait comme si elle était fille unique* (Mrs Dursley behaved as if she were an only child), Sarah reads *Madame Dursley faisait comme si elle était une fille unique* ... adding the indefinite article *une* that she would normally expect in this position. Of particular interest is the fact that, where the French text systematically refers to the Dursleys with their English titles of *Mr et Mrs*, Sarah equally systematically reads these titles as *monsieur et madame Dursley* wherever they occur in the text.

She also replaces some verb forms with ones that more commonly occur in conversation. In place of *Il n'était pas question que le petit Dudley se mette à fréquenter un enfant comme celui-là* (there was no question of little Dudley mixing with a child like that), she reads *Il n'était pas question que le petit Dudley se met a fréquenter un enfant comme celui-là*, replacing the subjunctive with the present tense. She frequently misreads the *imparfait* past tense as she did in the dual language books, for example: *possédant* for *possédaient*.

In her summary of part of the French text Sarah avoids using the past tense altogether:

Y a des voisins qui s'appellent Madame et Monsieur Dursley.... (long pause)... Ils aiment pas la sœur de Madame Dursley parce que ils croient que ils sont fous. Et, euh, ils aiment pas leur fils parce que ... cette famille fait honte, si les voisins vient pour voir, ils ont peur s'ils vont dire quelque chose.

(There are neighbours who are called Mrs and Mr Dursley... They don't like Mrs Dursley's sister because they think they are mad. And, er, they don't like their son because, that family embarrasses them, if the neighbours came to see, they are frightened they will say something.)

Strategies for working out meanings

Sarah reads fluently and understands the basic meaning. She and I go on to discuss some of the vocabulary in more detail. She tells me words she is not sure of and, in turn, I ask her about words I think she may not know. Her vocabulary is extensive. On the one hand there are fairly common words that she asks about: *diriger* (to direct), *fabriquer* (to make), *posséder* (to possess, to have). On the other hand I find that she knows more unusual and quite technical words like *entreprise* (business), *clôture* (fence), *espionner* (to spy) and *perceuse* (drill).

Her strategy with this text when faced with an unfamiliar word is to re-read the passage in French, use the context to work out the meaning and only refer back to the English to confirm her decision. In this way she works out *sornettes* (a story book word). Asked to guess she tries *nonsense*, and then finds that is exactly the word used in the English text.

Exploring issues in translation

Translations for publication in dual language books aim to follow the original text closely. The texts we are now working on are aimed for stand-alone publication. They are also more complex literary texts. Sarah is now exploring differences between the two versions. When asked about *craignaient*, she translates: 'they're scared!' She checks with the English and finds 'their greatest fear'. Similarly with *convaincus*. She offers 'convince', the correct translation. but struggles to find the equivalent in the English text and discovers it is simply 'think'.

As she reads on I realise the French text uses a different register from the English. There are many examples where the English text uses words that are common in everyday speech, but the French uses words more commonly encountered in books. For example, in English 'the boy was another good reason...' is translated as *son existence constituait une raison supplémentaire...* (his existence constituted an additional reason).

Possibly because it was rushed into publication, the translation into French of the Harry Potter is a little clumsy; it would not pass Lathey's 'read aloud' test (2006:10). The next text Sarah works on is *Little Women*. Perhaps because the French translation has a much higher literary quality and an easy rhythm, Sarah reads it more fluently. As she did with titles in the Harry Potter story, she gallicises the names of the characters, pronouncing Amy with a French A sound and Beth as *Bet*.

Sarah reads a paragraph in French, then the equivalent in English. She looks at a part of the text that reads in French '*Je trouve ça injuste, renchérit la benjamine*', and in English 'added little Amy, with an injured sniff'. She focuses on *la benjamine*, which is unfamiliar and finds 'added little Amy'. I suggest she compare *renchérit la benjamine* with 'added little Amy'. Sarah is struggling with my question, so I ask her how she would say 'little Amy' in French. She responds with *petite fille*. When asked directly what she thinks *la benjamine* means, she offers 'the youngest' which is exactly the meaning. She picks out *renchérit* (to go one better), and asks if it means 'sniffed'. I suggest 'If people were boasting and you made a bigger boast, you would *renchérit*'. We discuss what exactly 'added' and *renchérit* mean in the context of the story. Sarah notes that 'injured sniff' is not in the French text: 'there it says 'it's not fair''. Sarah notices that the French text is longer than the English and wonders whether the injured sniff was missed out 'maybe because they don't want too much writing on one page. It might be like the writer might think it is taking up the whole story.' Asked how she might demonstrate an injured sniff, Sarah responds in a dramatic whisper 'I don't think it's *fair*!'

Sarah has spotted a sentence which is quite different in French: '*Et elle soupira en pensant à toutes les jolies choses dont elle avait envie*' She focuses on '*soupira*' which does not feature in the English text, which reads as: 'she thought regretfully of all the pretty things she wanted'. Sarah is not sure how to interpret the difference because she does not know the meaning of *soupirer*. Then she suggests 'maybe 'regretfully' isn't a word in French, maybe they just wanted to change the words so it's different to the English text.' She explains 'Because when you're translating, some words won't mean the same, some words might not have the same meaning'. She becomes fascinated by the process of comparing the two texts and continues.

118

She is intrigued by *nouvelles partitions*, which is the French translation of 'new music'. She thinks the word might mean a tape, then she suggests 'the text of the songs and the notes', which is exactly what it means. She asks some questions about open fireplaces then works out that *la balayette à cendres* is for 'sweeping the hearth, bits of burnt coal'. She is very amused to find the metaphor *rat de bibliothèque* (library rat) and immediately figures out that it means 'bookworm'.

Retelling a story

I am keen to find out how Sarah handles the retelling of a shorter, well structured story. I offer her the bilingual version of *The Pied Piper* (Barkow, 2002). This text is similar in level of difficulty to the first texts that we read together, and it is a story she knows well. While she reads fluently and with expression in English, her miscues in French, are related to the pronunciation of verb forms. The story is told using the *passé simple*, a past tense used commonly in written narrative, but generally avoided in ordinary speech. The structure of French verbs is notoriously complex and French school children spend many years learning them. While Sarah mispronounces many of the verbs in the text, there is no question that she understands their meaning.

Sarah gets into role as a story teller:

> *Le joueur de flûte et il joue pour les gens de Hamelin pour que les rats sort de Hamelin. Et puis les rats part dans l'eau et ils meurent dans l'eau. Et puis le maire il veut pas payer d'argent. Et le joueur de flûte, parce que il dit il n'a pas fait du bien. Il a pris tous les enfants, tous les enfants à la colline. Avec sa flûte, parce que les enfants chanteront et dansaient à la musique. Et puis ils sont partis à la colline, mais il y avait un garçon qui ne pouvait pas bien marcher, et il pouvait pas partir avec eux. Et puis, quand il était revenu, tous les parents demandaient là où les autres enfants étaient. Et puis le garçon, il a expliqué tout ce qui se passait. Et puis les parents, ils criaient et pleurant pour leurs enfants qui étaient pas revenus.*

> (The Pied Piper and he plays for the people of Hamelin so that the rats will leave Hamelin. And then the rats go into the water and die in the water. And then the mayor, he doesn't want to pay any money. And the Pied Piper, because he said he didn't do any good. He took all the children, all the children to the hill. With his pipe, because the children sang and danced to the music. And then they went to the hill, but there was one boy who couldn't walk well, and he couldn't go with them. And then, when he came back, all the parents asked where all the other children were. And then the boy, he explained every-

thing that was happening. And then the parents, they shouted and wept for their children who had not come back.)

Sarah comments on the mayor's behaviour

Il est méchant, il est gourmand aussi. Parce que il pense tout le temps à l'argent' (He's nasty, he's greedy too. Because he always thinks about money), and on the piper's *'Il est un peu étrange. Parce que, ses habits, ça change les couleurs tout le temps. Il a emmené tous les enfants pour habiter avec lui. Dans la cave.*

(He's a bit strange. Because his clothes change colour all the time. He took all the children to live with him. In the cave.)

Having heard how much she likes writing stories in English, I prompt Sarah to think what might happen next, perhaps to imagine herself as one of the children. She immediately responds in role as one of the children in the story:

Il était resté avec nous, et puis il nous avait demandé si on voulait rentrer pour ... tous les enfants disent pas, parce que le maire, le monsieur, qui est méchant. ... Ils sont partis dans les rues pour le suivre. Ils sort de la caverne. ... to another town ... quand les parents essaient de chercher, ils ne peut pas les trouver dans l'autre ville parce que la porte de la caverne s'est déjà fermée. Ils grandiront dans la ville, et puis ils ont pensé qu'est-ce qu'il s'est passé à leurs parents... et pourtant (unclear) les parents, ils sont très tristes parce qu'ils ont plus de parents.

(He stayed with us, and then he asked us if we wanted to return to ... all the children didn't say, because the mayor, the man, he is nasty. They went into the streets to follow him. They came out of the cave ... to another town ... when their parents tried to find them, they couldn't find them in the other town because the door of the cave had already closed. They will grow up in the town, and then they wondered what happened to their parents ... and yet their parents (un-clear), they are very sad because they no longer have parents).

I ask her: *Et les parents sont tristes aussi?* (And their parents are sad too?) Sarah continues, and I am quite surprised at the turn her story takes:

Oui, à cause du joueur de flûte. Et le maire aussi....et le joueur de flûte ... moi je pense que c'est lui qui avait amené les rats, ... parce que je crois que c'est lui qui avait amené les rats, et si il les chasse encore, il aura de plus en plus d'argent. Parce que il avait dit, si le maire le paie pas il va faire beaucoup de choses méchantes à cette ville. Alors (unclear) c'est lui qui avait amené les rats (yes, because of the pied piper. And the mayor too, and the pied piper ... I think it was him who brought the rats ... because I think it was him who brought the rats, and if he chases them again, he will get more money. Because he said, if the mayor did not pay him, he would do lots of nasty things to the town. And so (unclear) it's him who brought the rats.)

By now Sarah is used to my asking her to do things in both languages and she is happy to start again, telling the story in English.

There's a Pied Piper and he comes to the town of Hamelin to get rid of all the rats. And then ... he said he would only get rid of all the rats if the mayor paid him twenty pieces of gold. And then the mayor said he would be pleased to pay if he got all the rats out of the town. So he played his flute and because it was beautiful music to the rats' ears, they all followed him. And then, when they got to the river Weser, the Pied Piper started making awful wailing noises in his pipe. And then all the rats drowned themselves into the river and died. And then the Pied Piper came back for his twenty pieces of gold and the mayor was a greedy man so he said he wouldn't like to pay, to pay him. But then the Pied Piper said, but you said you would pay me. And then they argued and then the Pied Piper shouted and said I'll bring more awful things in your town if you don't pay me. So, following after the (unclear)... the people were preparing their town, the Pied Piper got his pipe and started playing to the children. And then all the children heard and then more and more children came gathering round. Then he went to the hill and all the children followed him, one by one. Except a little boy who had crutches and he couldn't walk. When he came back he told all the people of Hamelin what had happened. They cried and shouted for their children, but they couldn't see them anywhere.

'That's the story in the book. Do you want to tell me in English again, what happened next?'

They went in the hill and then, they went in the cave and then they came out in another town. And the children grew up there and then they wondered why their parents left them, 'cos they couldn't remember. And then the parents might have discovered the cave and then they went in, and then the cave door shut and they were trapped in there for ever. And they couldn't see a way out. And then one day a boy said, we want to go back to our parents and the Pied Piper said, I'm afraid that can't be done. And they cried and shouted for their parents and the parents could hear them and they banged on the cave and they shouted but they couldn't get out.

'Oh, that's very dramatic! So what happened?'

The children didn't find them in the cave because they didn't know they were in there. And so they begged and pleaded with the Pied Piper to bring their parents back and then he said, you can't stay in that awful town because of the greedy mayor. And then soon Hamelin was just an empty town with no people left. That's the end.

Looking at Sarah's stories side by side I am struck by both the similarities and differences. Sarah's French story is shorter (388 words to 466 in English), which is a substantial difference, given that it generally takes more words to express the same idea in French than it does in English.

The sequence of events is similar in both versions. In both she recounts how the piper came to rid Hamelin of rats, how the rats drowned and how the mayor refused to pay. Both versions describe the children following the piper to the hill, the little boy left behind who tells the parents about the fate of their children, the parents crying for their children. Neither mentions the cavern into which the children disappear.

The English story provides much more detail: it describes the bargain struck between the piper and the mayor, the beauty and power of the music that lured the rats to their death, the argument between the mayor and the piper. While it is clear from the transcripts that Sarah is fluent in her narration in English, the greater detail may also be accounted for by the fact that she is more confident about the basic structure of the story, having already told it once.

The shorter narrative in French tempted me to ask her to develop the story further; I requested a similar extension to the English version. The major differences between her two narratives occur in this imagined continuation of the tale. In the English version the missing cavern plays a key role. While in both versions the children are trapped in it, then released to live in a different town, in the English version the parents, seeking their children, find the cavern and are trapped in it themselves, for ever, hearing their children but unable to be heard by them. In both versions of Sarah's story, the children miss their parents: in the English one they express a wish to return to their parents but are prevented from doing so by the piper; in the French version they just wonder what happened to their parents.

The French version extends beyond the point where the English narrative ends. Sarah develops a dramatic twist and explores the theory that the Pied Piper is the greater villain, that he has ruthlessly blackmailed and exploited the community to satisfy his own greed for money. Put together, the two stories, developed in parallel through two languages, provide a dramatic and sophisticated exploration of a traditional moral tale which ends in tragedy as

Sarah avoids the happy ending that many children like to add when developing such stories. I am curious to know whether Sarah's bilingualism provides her with a dual insight into possible underlying meanings of the tale.

Sarah writing

Sarah enjoys writing stories, but these are generally in English. Her teacher told me she had had little experience of writing in French. While she is clearly far less experienced as a writer than as a reader, her experience of reading seems to have helped her. Like most children writing independently, she invents her own spellings based on her understanding of the sound-spelling correspondence and word patterns that she has remembered. She avoids using accents.

After she had finished retelling the story of the Pied Piper, she suggested writing it. She settled to writing independently, in silence.

> *Une fois, il's aver une ville qui s'appela Hamelin. Beacoups de rats eter venue dans cet'e ville, le gents de Hamelin criant a le maire pour faire quelque chose, mais le maire criant aussi, en disant, 'Je ne peux rien faire. Je ne suis pas un chasseur de rats'. Apres un monsieur etrange eter venue dans leur ville. Il's demadent a le maire vingt pieces de argent, et si ils faisont sa, il's casseront tous les rats de cette ville. Le jouer de flute jouant sa flute, epuit touts les rats ant suivi jusque a la rivier Wesser, le jouer de flute comencer a fair be bruits qui etaits pas plaisents a les rats, et ils ce jetons se leau, enyourer.*

(Once there was a town called Hamelin. Lots of rats came into this town, the people of Hamelin shouted to the mayor to do something, but the mayor shouted too, saying I can't do anything, I am not a rat-catcher. Then a strange gentleman came to their town. He asked the mayor for twenty pieces of silver, and if they did that, he'll break all the rats in this town. The piper played his pipe and then all the rats followed him to the river Weser, the piper began to make a noise that was not nice for the rats and they threw themselves in the water, drowned.

The story did not get any further: Sarah had to stop when the lunch hour came and I had no further opportunity to meet her.

Her invented spellings are most in evidence in her verbs: *aves/aver* for *avait*; *eter* for *etait/etaient*; *ce* for *se*; *sa* for *ça*; *leau* for *l'eau* (water). The only spelling she has invented that doesn't represent accurately the sound of the word is *enyourer*, which I assume from the context means *noyer* (drowned).

The story is different again. But what intrigues me most about this story written in French is the fact that, in spite of some stylistic difficulties, it has more detail, like the earlier version told in English. Aspects of both oral tales come together in this third version.

I was seriously disappointed about the lack of opportunity for Sarah to complete her story. I would very much like to have known how she was planning to end it, which version she might have chosen, whether she would have blended them into one narrative and what she would have had to say about the role of the piper.

Discussion

The context in which Sarah was teaching herself to read was different from the other children's. While I had the benefit of sharing the same language there were no interactions for me to observe and I became a participant in the process, locating books and asking questions, a bit like Lere did with Albana.

The participation of Sarah's teacher in the Redbridge project provided a great opportunity for Sarah to extend her reading skills. The school which she and Lek and Durkan attended did not involve parents as directly in the programme as Magda and Albana's school did. However Sarah's teacher spoke French and was able to provide resources and much encouragement. My presence as a participant observer enabled Sarah to gain access to more advanced books in French. While the dual language books provided a starting point, by the time the research study ended she no longer needed the two texts to make meaning. In response to Sarah's enthusiasm for reading French, her father went searching and found more suitable books for her. She particularly liked the French version he found of *The Diary of Anne Frank*.

With respect to Sarah's identity as learner: of all the children in the project she was by far the most balanced bilingual. By the end of the study her reading skills in French were developing rapidly and, if she continued to have access to advanced texts, should eventually catch up with her English. The writing was more problematic. The complex verb system used in formal written French poses a challenge. Sarah had made a good start but would benefit from feedback from a teacher to develop further. A 'fast-track' option at secondary school would be particularly beneficial.

Of Sarah's identity as a person I got to know a lot less. She is older than the other children and much more reserved. While an excellent reader and writer, her mathematic skills are very poor and this affects her progress in school. Although I never saw any aspect of this, I was informed that she had a quick temper and was quite frequently in trouble in school because of this. I met her on her own; I had no opportunity to observe her interacting with other children. We discussed text. She volunteered little information about herself that wasn't directly related to literacy. She was very pleased when I was able to offer her a dual language picture book published in Lingala and French but this did not prompt any personal discussion. I was very aware that, although I share her language, I did not share her cultural background as a British French-speaking Congolese.

Children with a substantial experience of literacy and an analytic approach to reading can teach themselves to read with comparatively little assistance. The relationship between French and English makes the transfer of skills fairly easy. The languages share the Roman alphabet. The language structure of simple sentences is not very dissimilar and, due to the influence of Latin and Norman French on English, there are many cognates. Having learned to read in French before she started school, Sarah was rapidly able to work out how to read English. I remember going through the same process myself at the age of 6 and playing with words and phrases across languages as Sarah does.

Sarah was very interested in the way in which the same concept was expressed differently and was aware of the different range of meaning that words have in different languages. The big question that Sarah raised for me was the possibility that, given those shifts in meaning, encountering a story simultaneously in two languages might encourage a deeper exploration of the underlying meaning. I left her hoping that her experiences in secondary school would enable her to explore and develop her story telling and writing skills and to fulfil her biliterate promise.

9

Mohammed – learning to read in Gujarati

Mohammed, like Mydda, has a new script to learn. Whereas she starts with working out the letters and trying to solve the puzzle presented by the Urdu script, he approaches the problem from a very different angle. This chapter follows Mohammed as he explores the language of stories with his mother, retells them in his own way, works out word meanings across languages, and begins to engage with the Gujarati script.

The Gujarati script has developed from the Devanagari script and is written from left to right. The writing system is syllabic. This means that all consonants include a vowel sound; vowels can be written as separate letters or as diacritics attached to a consonant.

Language and literacy

Mohammed is 7 years old. His father was born and educated in London and speaks a dialect of Gujarati, spoken in the rural area from which his family originate and commonly used in the east London community where he lives. Mohammed's father can speak and read Urdu and read in Arabic, but never had the opportunity to learn to read Gujarati. Mohammed's mother is a more recent arrival. She was educated in India in Gujarati and speaks the standard variety. She also learned Farsi and English at school and studied Urdu and Arabic at the Madressa.

Mohammed's parents are very keen that their children should grow up to be speakers of Gujarati and they use the language a great deal at home. Mohammed is in the same class as Magda and Albana and benefited from the same language support that was offered to all bilingual children by the teacher. Dual language books in Gujarati and English were available for

Mohammed to take home, and more could be obtained from the local library. The family also have access to television programmes in Gujarati and Mohammed is especially fond of anything historical. A teacher comes to the family home twice a week after school to instruct Mohammed and his 4 year old sister in Arabic and Qur'anic studies. Mohammed has also begun to learn French at school and enjoys trying out a few phrases with the researcher. He is confident and articulate, a fluent reader in English, and seems very comfortable in the research situation.

His mother Farhana has focused on the oral development of the language, telling and reading stories to her children. While Mohammed is familiar with the script from the dual language books, at the start of the observations described in this chapter he had only just begun to become aware of letters and cannot yet identify or name any. However he describes as reading the way in which he and his mother work with the books.

Farhana invited the researcher to observe her reading with him at home. After school and a snack with his sister, he curls up on the sofa with his mother and they choose books together. His younger sister attends nursery at the same school. She plays on the carpet, at the computer, or uses the coffee table for drawing and colouring. She occasionally vies for her mother's attention, and is keen to show the researcher that she loves books and is learning to read.

Reading together

Unlike Mydda in Urdu, Mohammed is a confident speaker of Gujarati. He approaches the task from a completely different angle. Where Mydda uses bottom-up strategies, tackling the Urdu script as a puzzle to be solved, Mohammed hasn't yet engaged with the duality of the text on the page. In essence he is still operating orally, focusing on the overall meaning of the text and of individual words in context. When it comes to showing his understanding of the range of meaning of words, he provides both translations and definitions in English. This is what reading in Gujarati means to him.

The first text that Farhana and Mohammed read together in the presence of the researcher is *The Raja's Big Ears* (Desai, 1989). Farhana has read the story to Mohammed several times in Gujarati and he is very familiar with it. He has also read the English many times by himself. Another favourite is *The Naughty Mouse* (Stone, 1989). When Mohammed is offered a choice of how he wants to read a story he asks his mother to read the text first in Gujarati and then he follows with an English reading. Occasionally he reverses the process and reads first in Gujarati from memory.

Farhana's strategy to develop understanding and vocabulary as she reads in Gujarati, is to stop at intervals in her reading and ask questions about the meaning of words. Mohammed switches confidently between Gujarati and English. Farhana seems intent on focusing him on individual words, to get precision in his thinking. In response to the presence of an English speaking researcher, she asks her questions in English, expecting a translation into Gujarati.

The following is an example of the many lengthy exchanges between Farhana and Mohammed as they read from a dual language book. Mohammed has picked up *The Naughty Mouse* and he directs the structure of the session, telling his mother exactly how he wants to read with her: 'you say it in Gujarati first, then I say it in English and I say the words you said in Gujarati. You ask me.'

> Farhana: (Reading page 1 of the story) *Shambhado balako.*
>
> Mohammed: Listen children.
>
> Farhana: There was one...
>
> Mohammed (interrupting): *Balako* means children and *shambhado* means listen.
>
> Farhana: OK. There was once a very naughty and cunning mouse. Oh, sorry! I was supposed to read... *ek khoob mastikhor ne chalaak oonder hato.*
>
> Mohammed: There was once a very naughty and cunning mouse.
>
> Farhana: OK.
>
> Mohammed: *Oonder* means mouse.
>
> Farhana: *Te tamesha koi ne koi masti karay rakhato.*
>
> Mohammed: He always, he was always looking for mischief.

As his mother reads the Gujarati, Mohammed listens intently, then responds with the English version from the book, by glancing occasionally at the text or from memory. He is keen to demonstrate his understanding by picking out individual words and phrases for translation.

> Farhana (Reading page 2): *Ek divas tenay vichaar karyo.*
>
> Mohammed: *Ek* means one, day means *divas*. *Ek*, one day he thought to himself.
>
> Farhana: *Hoon shahayrma jayish.*
>
> Mohammed: I'll go into town. *Shahayr* means town.
>
> Farhana: *Aakho divas hoon gharmaa rahi kantali gayo choon.*
>
> Mohammed: With staying in my home all day.
>
> Farhana: I am fed up...

Mohammed: I am fed up with staying in my home all day. Fed up is *kantali gayo.*

Farhana: *Chomaasane lithey bahoo samay soothei ander rahayvoo padyu chay.*

Mohammed: The monsoons have kept me in too long. *Bahoo divas* means too long.

Mohammed says *bahoo divas*, which means long day, instead of repeating *bahoo samay*, a long time.

Farhana. Mmm. (Reading from page 3) *Aa mastikhor oonder kapda pahayri shaher taraf jawa oopadiyo.*

Mohammed: So the naughty mouse got dressed and set out for the town. *Kapdoo* means dressed.

Mohammed uses *kapdoo*, which means a dress or dress fabric. Although the correct response would have been *pahayri*, to wear, what Mohammed says makes sense in this context.

Farhana: *Rastamaa nachto koodato ay jato hato tiya teni nazar ek moti kapadni dookaan par padi.*

Mohammed: As he skipped happily along the road he came across a big shop which sold cloth. Skipped means *nackay* and shop means *dookan.*

This time Mohammed introduces a new word, *nackay*, which is not in the text, and which means dance, rather than repeating *koodato* (skipping).

Farhana: *Dookaandaar tayj vakhatay dookaanmaa jato hato.*

Mohammed: The shopkeeper was just going into his shop.

Farhana: (Now reading from page 5) *Mastikor oonder chaanomaano tayni pachar gayo.*

Mohammed: (Reading from page 4) Naughty mouse crept quietly behind him. Him means, euh... does it begin with...?

Farhana: *Tani pachar gayo* (went behind him). OK? *Dookaandaarnay tayni khabhar nahoti...*

Mohammed: (interrupting) Behind means *pachar!*

Farhana: Behind means *pachar*, that's right.

Mohammed: The shopkeeper didn't know he was there.

Farhana: *Jayro thay bhaydho ke tayne oonderne aynisaamay joyo.*

Mohammed: (yawning) As he sat down he saw the mouse in front of him, in front of him. In front means *aggadi.*

Farhana: *Maari dookanmaa too shoon karay chay?*

Mohammed: Run away, said the man, what are you doing in my shop?

Although Mohammed is listening intently to his mother, he is not following the Gujarati script on the page, nor is Farhana pointing to it. His strategy to demonstrate his understanding is to provide translations of words and phrases that his mother has just used, taking the initiative and choosing these words himself. On a number of occasions the words he picks out are not actually the ones his mother used, which suggests that, rather than simply parroting his mother, he is more intent on the meaning of the sentence than on the precise words used; he translates this into his own Gujarati which, as his mother explained, is often non-standard (for example when he says *bahoo divas* instead of *bahoo samay*). Farhana has clearly noted this: after that particular substitution she says 'mmm', but chooses not to comment, as all his responses, while not in standard Gujarati, make sense in context and reflect his own usage.

Strategies

When asked to talk about the strategies she uses to teach Mohammed, Farhana refers to 'drilling in his head all the words'. While this may indeed be her intention, her strategies for doing so are rather more creative and varied than this comment suggests. They include reading the story several times, talking to him about it, encouraging him to anticipate what is going to happen, asking questions, providing definitions in both languages, translating backwards and forwards between both languages, emphasising key words, demonstrating words through mime and even a little playing school. The following section provides evidence from the transcripts of some of the strategies used.

Talking about the story

As she opens *The Raja's Big Ears* at the page that shows elephants carrying tree trunks from the jungle, Farhana asks: 'Now what's happening?' Mohammed offers 'Oh, elephants are picking it up and they're gonna take it to, um, make it paper'. Farhana responds 'Make it paper. You do make paper from wood. But here, it's not going to happen.' Mohammed seems to have forgotten 'What are they going to do with it?' Farhana encourages him 'You know this story, what's happened with the wood?' Mohammed remembers 'Ah, yeah, yeah, yeah! Um, they, I think they make instruments'. Farhana agrees but waits for him to remember the rest 'they do make instruments after' and Mohammed responds excitedly 'Then they chopped it all into logs and hired an elephant and took the logs to a factory, where he sold them for a *lot* of money!'

A little later, while Farhana attends to his little sister Zainab who has crashed the computer, Mohammed enjoys telling me that he knows what is going to happen:

> then the Raja invites everybody to a party and then, you know, all the instruments, the first instrument said 'Raja's got big ears' and then the tabla and then the tabla said 'Who told you? Who told you?' and then the tambourine says 'Manji told us'. And then after, he, um, he got Manji and he said 'please forgive me' and then after, at the end, he, he, ... *indistinct*... there shouldn't be any king, and he forgive the, he forgive Manji. And he threw the hat away! He threw the topee away.

I ask him: 'So what about his ears? Did he still have big ears?' and Mohammed explains 'Yeah, he didn't want to mention them.'

Defining words

Both Farhana and Mohammed use translations and definitions. The nearest that Farhana comes to drilling is the way she emphasises key words which she thinks may be less familiar to him: *bhaday* means hire; *paisa* means money; she asks 'chopped?' To which Mohammed responds '*katkaa!*'

Because of the way in which his mother phrases a question, Mohammed sometimes attempts a definition of the word in English, as follows:

> Farhana: (reads page 1) *Rajanay thatu kay praja teni maskaree kersay thaythee tay hamesha kaan topee pahayree rakhto.*
>
> Mohammed reads the English text: he always wore a topee to cover them as he thought his subjects would laugh at him if they saw them.
>
> Farhana: What is subject mean?
>
> Mohammed: Subject means like, um, some things, subjects means like, similar to objects, but subjects are like, euh, things what you do.
>
> Farhana: Yeah, but here subjects means, it's *preja,* some say this is my kingdom and this is the people, the people who live in raja's kingdom. That is subject, OK?
>
> Mohammed: Mmm.

From the exchange above it is clear that Mohammed has a good vocabulary in English, he knows the words *subject* and *object* and makes the connection between them. However the subject he is thinking of is 'things what you do', like subjects studied in school.

Farhana agrees with his definition, explains that in this text the meaning is different, offers both the Gujarati word and an explanation in English and checks 'that is subject, OK?'

On the next page, when Mohammed reads 'But the Raja had warned him to never say a word to anyone' (deviating slightly from the text which reads 'him never to say'), Farhana asks him 'What is warn mean?'

This time Mohammed struggles with an English definition: 'Warn means, um, to not, um, warn means ...', gives up and supplies the word in Gujarati, *kayhu*, indicating that he is clear about the meaning.

On the following page, when Mohammed reads about the 'wide, tall tree', Farhana asks 'what is wide mean, wide?' Again Mohammed responds with both the Gujarati and an English definition '*Maktu*, and it means like it's not narrow, it's, and it's ...' Farhana confirms: 'you said it in Gujarati, wide means *maktu*, yes.'

Demonstrating

As well as asking questions and placing particular emphasis on new words, Farhana sometimes demonstrates physically. She reads from *The Raja's Big Ears* then asks '*muwy shoo khackay like palathi wadinay – palathi?* (what's Mummy saying? like sit cross-legged, cross-legged?). What does cross-legged mean, Mohammed?' and she demonstrates on the sofa 'We do it like that.'

Later in the same text when discussing how the wood from the jungle was turned into instruments Farhana asks 'What is *lakri?*' Mohammed shouts excitedly 'wood!', then she asks '*Tabla?* That is the problem. I told you' and she demonstrates drumming on her knees. Mohammed immediately understand, 'Oh, drum, yeah, drum. You play it with your hands.'

Playing school

Following on from the demonstration of the word cross-legged, Farhana and Mohammed are still sitting that way next to each other on the sofa. After a very lively sequence of reading in English from Mohammed, Farhana says in a teacherly voice 'let me ask you a few more questions here. It says, now listen, you have to listen to me carefully, because I'm going to ask you a question, OK? *Hay vrux maray thanay aa kahaywooj padsay.*'

Mohammed is immediately in role, he waves his hand in the air excitedly and calls out 'Miss, he's saying that 'tree, I must tell you this''. Farhana shows her approval 'Well done'.

Retelling the story

Mohammed has spontaneously retold stories, to his mother or to me in English. While initially keen to tell them in Gujarati, he now seems a little reluctant and the expression on his face suggests that he does find it harder. However he loves the story of *The Naughty Mouse*. He wants to retell it in English. Farhana suggests: 'OK, first in English, then in Gujarati.' She prompts him 'He went into the tailor's shop and then he said to the tailor 'I want you to make a beautiful cap for me...'

Mohammed starts retelling:

> *Anay kahyoo kay manay ek soonder cap joaye. May ni karo, may ni karo, may ni karo, karvano ki ni karrano. 'Ni karvano' oonder* began to lose his temper. *Mai* soldier *sathay aawoo raatna. 'Ni, ni mai ek topi banawoo' anay* mirror *ma joyo. Aa* plain *a chay manay sequins joaye toe ay* sequins *na shopmaa gayo. Anay* shopkeeper *nay kahyoo 'manay* sequins *joay'. 'Ni, ni mai nahi aapoo toe ay kahyo' toe mai raatna* soldier *saathay aawoo* shopkeeper *kay, 'ni, ni, may* sequins *aapoo* different colour*ni', nay mai shoo karvaroo tanay.*

> (and said that I want a beautiful cap. 'Are you going to make me one or not? 'I won't make'. 'You won't do?' the mouse said. 'At night I'll come with soldiers.' 'No, no I will make a cap,' and he looked in the mirror. 'It's plain. I want sequins in it.' So he went to the sequins shop and said to the shopkeeper, 'I want sequins'. 'No, no, I won't give you.' Then he said again, 'I'll come with soldiers'. The shopkeeper said 'no, no, I will give sequins of different colours'.

Mohammed continues:

> *Oonder kahyoo shopkeeper nay, manay* cloth *joyay. Ni mai nai apoon tanay shooperay kahyoo. Too many aapwanokeni aapwano* to mouse *kay* shopkeeper*nay 'mai ratna* soldier *saathay aawoo'. 'ni, ni mai* cloth *apoo tanay.'*

> (The mouse told the shopkeeper 'I want a cloth'. 'No I won't give you', the shopkeeper said. 'Are you going to give me or not?' Then the mouse says to the shopkeeper 'At night I will come with the soldiers'. 'No, no, I will give you the cloth.'

Mohammed continues retelling the story in the same manner.

Grapho-phonic and word level work

Near the end of the first observation session, Mohammed and his mother look through an old and attractively presented Gujarati school primer which is basically about numbers, but has letters as well and is also a colouring book. It is interesting that for all the hours he has spent with his mother reading from dual language books, Mohammed does not seem to have taken a lot of notice of individual letter shapes. Farhana explains that she hadn't really started on this.

As I find him staring at a page of letters in sequence I ask him in what way he thinks they are different. 'They're symbols, I think they're symbols,' he tells me confidently, pointing to them. Once again I am impressed with his confident use of vocabulary in English.

As he looks intently at the letter shapes and copies some of them, it becomes apparent that he is really unfamiliar with them. He comments on the ways in which some of them resemble English letters.

'That looks like an F to me'. To which Farhana responds, describing the letter's sound, 'It's not an F, it's a K'. He tries again That looks like a L' and Farhana starts to explain that the letter looks like it does because it has a symbol attached to it that indicates a vowel sound.

Mohammed looks again at the list of Gujarati letters and points to the first one in the sequence 'That must be A, is this B then?' and Farhana has to explain that the letters are not in the same sound sequence as in English (ie ABC).

Mohammed copies the letter that sounds R (which he thinks looks a bit like the number 2) with the attachment for the vowel A. He picks up *The Raja's Big Ears* and looks on the first page for Gujarati words that begin with that combination. Farhana guides him 'Can you find R for me? In the third line.' 'Darling, in the first line, can you find R?' 'Another line. First line only, look on this first line, this line here.' Mohammed finds it 'Ra, yeah! YEEEAAAH!' and he punches the air in triumph. Mohammed and his mother continue to look for well known words and he tries to identify distinctive consonants.

On my second visit Mohammed is again playing this letter identification game, still partly trying to guess from the resemblance some letters have to

English ones. Farhana starts explaining about double letters and how vowels are written as part of the consonant unless they begin the word. Mohammed starts rolling sounds around in his mouth with great pleasure '*Tschuh! Tschuh! Titch. Tsch! Tsch! Eeeee!*'

On my third visit Mohammed proudly demonstrates that, not only can he recite all the numbers to fourteen in Gujarati, but he can also correctly identify the symbols that represent them. He is exploring writing his own name (not the pseudonym used in this text) and trying to understand the sequence and the sounds of the letters. He has found the first letter then looks around and asks 'A and I !!! But where's A and I?' and Farhana explains 'We don't do A and I in Gujarati. What we do is put two signs on top ... no, all you need to do is put two signs, you know when we do it in Arabic? Zabba. So that's two zabbas'. Mohammed, who is learning Arabic with his home tutor, immediately knows what she means 'two zabbas!' Farhana guides him 'On top! On top! There, two zabbas'. Mohammed writes painstakingly.

On my fourth visit he proudly shows me that he has written the names of all family members on a sheet of paper, as well as the pseudonym that he has chosen.

Mohammed

The writing is confident and I am much impressed. He then proceeds to explain the spelling of his real name to me 'That's the zed, and the two vowels are A and I are them two lines'.

Farhana comments that Mohammed's understanding was greatly helped by the book *The Fisherman and the Cat* (Ashraf, 2007), which she had originally put aside for later as the story is quite sophisticated. The dual language story was written specifically for second generation speakers of Gujarati in the UK who want to learn the language of their community. It includes information on the writing system and on vocabulary, as well as an audio CD. Farhana explains that, for children who really want to be literate:

> this is a really good book... First I thought it's going to be a little harder for him
> to explain all these (referring to the script). Then again they have the words as

well, and Gujarati and English words. The story is much more advanced, so I thought I might as well leave it for now. Then he was keeping on asking me about the words and letters and all that and I thought, hang on a minute, we do have this book, and it's got all the explanation what you need really.

Accent and dialect

Farhana raised the issue of accent, dialect and standard Gujarati. She explained that, while Mohammed is reasonably fluent in Gujarati, he shares the accent and dialect spoken by his father and by many of the children he plays with in the community. Farhana herself is keen that he should learn the standard language, especially in the context of books. She explains that she welcomes the use of formal and literary terminology where it occurs in dual language books, as it provides her with an opportunity to widen Mohammed's vocabulary.

The following extract shows her demonstrating exactly that point, using the text of *The Raja's Big Ears*. Mohammed reads in English from page 2 'He would tell his secret to a tree' and Farhana asks him how he would express this in Gujarati. Mohammed responds with '*ay, ay kayhwa, kayhwano* tree', seemingly not having picked up the formal *vrux* word for tree. Farhana explains 'Tree means *vrux, jhaad, jhaad*', providing both the literary and the common words that he knows. He repeats '*jhaad. Ay kayhwano* tree' (again ignoring the word *vrux*). Farhana then reads on in Gujarati '*Ek vrux net ay khang waaf karshey*' (he would tell his secret to a tree) and, this time, Mohammed repeats exactly '*Ek vrux net ay khang waaf karshey*'. In the same sentence Farhana corrects his use of the colloquial *karo* (do) and offers *gayo* (went).

Earlier, when he is reading from the same page, Farhana corrects Mohammed's pronunciation. As he starts retelling a sentence, *Ek do Manji* ... (one day Manji) Mohammed uses a form of shortening the word that is common in his dialect. Farhana corrects him: *ek divas Manji*. But, oblivious, as many young children are whose grammar is corrected, he continues, *ek do Manji...*

Code-switching

Code-switching is a common form of informal speech among bilinguals. When children are dominant in English, the most common form of switching in a situation such as this, retelling a story, is for English words to be inserted into Gujarati phrases (Sneddon and Patel, 2003). Farhana explains the choice of words in different contexts.

> Normally, when we're home, I'm not going to use that *vajintra* (instrument) in Gujarati. I use 'instruments' in English anyway when I'm talking to them. But this is an opportunity for him to learn a different word.' The same rule applies to the word 'tree'. 'Every day, it's going to be 'tree' (in English). Yes, but when, if they know it, when we go to India, they would say, for 'tree' *jhaad*, but in a book, it's not going to be *jhaad*, it's going to be *vrux*.

When Mohammed uses 'walk', Farhana prompts him in Gujerati. In the context of working from the dual language book, Mohammed can prompt himself by reading the English text, but he also uses Gujarati words from memory alone. When retelling in English, although he generally reads the text, or recites it accurately from memory without looking at the page (being very familiar with the story), he sometimes switches into Gujarati. So, for example he says '*Ek do, ek do Manji* went for a walk in the jungle to think in peace and quiet. Suddenly he had the answer. He would tell his secret to *ek* tree', apparently reading from the text, but replacing 'one day' with *ek do*, and the article before 'tree' with *ek*.

Discussion and new developments

The way in which Mohammed and his mother approach learning to read in Gujarati is fundamentally different from that of the other children in this study. In many ways the challenge presented to him by the different script is similar to that faced by Mydda. He is highly articulate and well read in English and, unlike Mydda, he has always loved reading. Had Gujarati used the Roman script, one might have expected Mohammed to be one of those children, like Sarah, who can operate the transfer of reading skills effectively from one language to another by themselves.

Teachers who have taught children to read are familiar with the many different skills required and the controversies, as different approaches advocate different emphases and starting points. Mydda's mother starts with the small shapes, the letters on the page and how they combine to produce sounds, the approach known to many teachers as the synthetic, bottom-up approach. This is the approach used in many countries, including Pakistan, in which the sound-symbol relationship is regular. Farhana's strategy in teaching Mohamed is very different. All her attention is on the big shapes, the analytic top-down approach, the structures and the language of story, the meaning, the context (Goodman, 1996). Hers is the bed-time story model advocated by Holdaway (1979), the real books approach. She is teaching him to read in Gujarati in the way that many parents teach reading to their children, teaching him to love stories and to become familiar with the language of story in

Gujarati. She creates a warm, comfortable and positive environment for reading and is sensitive in the way she corrects and encourages Mohammed.

In the course of the observations, Farhana displays a variety of strategies for ensuring Mohammed's understanding of the text she reads to him. At the point at which the study started, he had not yet engaged with the script and I got the impression he was a little daunted by the prospect. While he expressed some curiosity about them, he seemed reluctant to engage with the symbols and the principles of Gujarati spelling. He seemed to be searching for a key, an easy correspondence, either, like the younger children described by Kenner, by exploring similarities in form between Gujarati and English letters, or by trying to find a sequence that matches the English ABC. Farhana realises that he is failing to engage with the syllabic nature of the Gujarati script and tries to help him by drawing analogies with the way in which vowels are represented in Arabic, the language which he is beginning to learn for religious purposes with a private tutor.

Mohammed gives the impression of someone who is comfortable in the English world of school where his good reading skills and his sophisticated use of the English language are fully appreciated. He is also a confident speaker of Gujarati who seizes the many opportunities to use the language with family and friends. He has relatives close by and there are a good many Gujarati Muslims in his environment who share his way of life. The interest taken in his language at school, the commitment of his mother and the attention of the researcher provide a positive reinforcement. Although he has not visited Gujarat, he has received visits from members of his family.

Mohammed's learner identity seems strongly focused around the pride he takes in his linguistic competence. This may be one of the reasons why he has been slow to engage with the printed word in Gujarati. One senses some frustration at being deskilled in the face of print in Gujarati, when the printed word is so transparent to him in English

With respect to identity, an interesting side story is provided by his little sister Zainab. When I first started visiting, Farhana told me that she was disappointed that Zainab seemed to have little interest in learning Gujarati. During my observations, Zainab would occasionally try to deflect attention from her brother, either by demanding her mother's attention, or by engaging directly with me, showing me a book or a picture. On two occasions I recorded her telling me her favourite story, *The Three Billy Goats Gruff* (Barkow, 2001b). I made sure I brought a dual language version of this on my next visit. In the course of a follow-up visit, some months after the last formal observations, Farhana told me how Zainab, now 5 years old, was in class with the teacher who had started the dual language reading programme in school and was now much more interested in Gujarati. On the basis of her offering to read to me, I could tell she was also developing her brother's talent for literacy in English.

At the end of the observation period, Mohammed and his mother were offered a Talking Pen with recorded versions of *The Three Billy Goats Gruff* in Gujarati and English to accompany the book. He was greatly excited by this and explored it at great length, exclaiming 'now I don't need my Mum all the time!' and explaining that he would now be able to read the Gujarati text whenever he felt like it. The Talking Pen and the Recorder Pen both became available to the researcher late in the study. A follow up is being considered to explore the impact on children's learning of the greater autonomy it might offer in gaining access to the lesser known language version. This may be particularly beneficial to Mohammed who takes such pride in being an independent reader.

10
Bilingual books – biliterate children?

This book set out to explore how children interact with text when they are reading simultaneously in two languages; to relate this to research relevant to the use of dual language books; and to place it in the rich and varied context in which such texts have been developed and used over the last thirty years; all in the hope that it may provide some assistance to teachers in supporting and developing children's languages and introducing new ones to their classroom.

The field work started in 2006 at a time when educational policy was becoming more bilingual friendly, when the teaching of languages in primary schools was developing, dual language books and resources were becoming available in an ever widening range of languages and teachers were trying out innovative ways of using them in the classroom. While there was very little research directly into the use of dual language texts, a handful of very active researchers in the UK were exploring the literacy practices of multilingual communities.

As the project developed, the educational context became ever more positive towards the languages spoken in children's families. At the time of writing this concluding chapter, the research context has been enriched by ongoing work on aspects of bilingual learning, on collaborations between mainstream and complementary schools and on language pedagogy in the primary classroom. Even the terminology is changing: from 'community languages' to 'our languages', 'world languages' or 'languages of the wider world'.

Four questions led the case studies described in this book. The transfer of skills from English to the family language was evident in all the cases, though it operated differently for Urdu and Gujarati compared to languages that use the Roman script. Metalinguistic understanding was most readily revealed in the Turkish study and comprehension in the French one. Issues of personal identity were more apparent in the Albanian, Turkish and Urdu studies.

The study at its beginning was informed by the work of Viv Edwards and Ming-Tsow and inspired by action research carried out by colleagues in east London schools. It revealed the great individuality of children's approaches to learning bilingually and, as always, it raised more questions than it answered.

The children's linguistic competence, the language priorities and patterns of use in the families, their funds of knowledge, the literacy resources available to them, the children's learning and adult teaching styles, all of these interacted to create the distinctive way in which each of the subjects approached the task of learning to read.

The history of dual language book use, the research into biliteracy reviewed in Chapter 2 and the case studies suggest ways in which such learning can be supported and developed in a range of contexts. The books provide a valuable starting point, especially for teachers who work in classes in which many languages are spoken, and they can create a bridge into bilingual learning. As children learn to explore languages collaboratively in the classroom, additional materials acquired from children's homes, the internet, complementary schools, community bookshops or language teaching courses for children can be added to the class resources. The latest research by Kenner *et al* (2008b) has demonstrated how children can be supported by both monolingual and bilingual adults, with help from their parents, to learn bilingually in the classroom. This provides children with the opportunity to use both their languages simultaneously to discuss texts or carry out tasks. As well as providing linguistic enrichment it enables children to make full use of their cognitive abilities, leading to a deeper understanding of both the issues studied and language itself.

There is a great deal of scope for both academic and classroom-based action research into children learning bilingually: into the pedagogy, the strategies, the resources that inspire children to succeed in different settings and circumstances. Action research networks empower teachers to try out new ideas, to explore and evaluate their own practice, to share experiences with colleagues and so create a base of evidence of strategies that are effective in the classroom.

Funded academic research (such as that carried out recently by Gregory and Kenner), while still classroom-based, is also needed so that the questions that led the present study may be explored more systematically. It would buy observation time and enable the employment of skilled and experienced research staff (who may also be teachers) who can interact with children in the language of their choice and use a wider range of instruments to explore the children's understanding than was possible in the present study.

The children who participated in this study had few opportunities to learn the language of the home and families had few resources to support them. The study confirmed the key role played by schools and individual teachers in empowering children, as Cummins suggests, by building on their knowledge, skills and personal identities, by providing language learning opportunities and by building partnerships with families and communities. It also revealed the great creativity, enthusiasm and persistence that children brought to the task of learning their languages and the pride they took in their identity as bilinguals.

Developing biliteracy in multilingual classrooms

The following suggestions will work effectively in classrooms in which many different languages are spoken. While most of these can be supported by teachers who do not share the languages of the children, they can be developed in many directions and enriched by bilingual teachers or through working in partnership with parents, complementary school teachers, bilingual adults or older children.

- **Resourcing** the classroom in multilingual material is an essential starting point: dual language books, literacy materials from children's homes or available in the community (such as books, primers, posters, newspapers and magazines), displays, games and multimedia material and website resources such as Language of the Month, CDs, DVDs and Talking or Recorder Pens. Actually using these materials in teaching will remove the 'English only' sign from the classroom and there are many ideas for doing this in *Learning and Teaching for Bilingual Children in the Primary Years* and other references listed in the Appendix.

- **Encouraging parents** to read with their children in the language of the home as well as in English. Good advice on how to set up this process is available from the Redbridge *Developing Reading Skills through Home Language Project*. A good starting point is to arrange a meeting of interested parents (or grandparents or siblings), to get to know about families' language use and preferences and offer resources and advice as necessary, but bearing in mind that the best schemes allow parents and children to address their own language priorities, learning styles and incorporate their own resources. Even if only one or two families are interested in the project it is worth supporting. If several families become involved, a regular meeting is helpful to share ideas, resources and momentum. Lists of suitable websites can be circulated. Where families do not have access to the internet, children can be supported to choose and print materials in the family language to take home.

■ **Awareness of language activities** in the classroom for all children, working in pairs or small groups, comparing languages and making hypotheses about how language works. There are many recommended ideas and resources from *Learning and Teaching for Bilingual Children in the Primary Years*, the *Framework for Languages*, Language of the Month, *March is Multilingual Month* and other materials listed in the Appendix. Dual language books are particularly useful in this context, at all different levels: monolingual children or children new to the language exploring the features of texts; children working with a partner who knows the language; children like Lek and Durkan, helping each other to read; advanced readers like Sarah working with a partner to explore more advanced features of text.

■ **Making bilingual books**: Many ideas for doing this were mentioned in Chapter 1. This activity has been found by all who have tried it to be highly motivating for children. It strongly supports literacy development in both languages, and creates personal texts that are greatly valued by children and their families, as demonstrated by the success of Identity Texts (see Cummins *et al*, 2006) and Magda and Albana's books in Albanian and English. Book making can be organised in classroom writing workshops, with support from bilingual adults if available, and from families at home, as a joint project with complementary school teachers, whether or not they can work physically in the same classroom. They can also be run as bilingual family learning projects. For children at the early stages of learning to write in another language, a bilingual shared writing activity is popular: after a story has been told and dramatised in two languages, two adults work with groups of children to produce parallel versions of the story through shared writing which can then be illustrated and displayed as story posters in the classroom. Books made by children can become a resource in the school library and be made available to a wider audience on the school website.

Reading strategies

The strategies that work best will vary according to the language experience and competence of children as well as the relationship between English and the family language. Children from families recently arrived in the UK are quite likely to have a good level of oral competence in the latter, although their use of it may decline significantly once they start school, as it did for Magda and Albana. Second and third generation children, as Kenner found, are much more likely to be dominant in English and may have very varied levels of competence in the family language. There may be several languages or language varieties used in the home for different purposes, not all of which will be used for literacy. Parents' literacy skills in community languages and in English will vary depending on their immigration trajectories and educational experiences.

The transferability of skills is at its easiest when the family language uses the Roman script, the children have a good level of oral competence and are good readers for their age in English. This was the case for Magda and Albana and the strategies used by their mothers worked well. They included:

- regular reading to the children in both languages
- initial instruction in the graphophonic system (which is regular in Albanian)
- scaffolding and discreet prompting and an initial focus on decoding the Albanian text
- encouraging repeated readings
- asking questions, discussing meanings and exploring the context of words in both languages
- using the English text for verification, comparison and discussion of meaning in English
- making use of clues such as illustrations and children's knowledge of stories for prediction
- when the opportunity presented itself, finding Albanian texts, teaching the children poems
- supporting the children in learning to write and make their own books.

The strategies include both top-down and bottom-up, make use of those the girls have used to learn to read in English, with an initial focus on decoding, which is appropriate given the nature of the Albanian writing system.

Where the family language uses a script that is different from English and children's knowledge of the spoken language is less secure, strategies need to be different.

The strategies used by Farhana were effective in helping Mohammed, who is a highly proficient reader in English, become more fluent in Gujarati, particularly in the language of story. These included:

- regular reading of stories in both languages
- asking Mohammed to read after her in Gujarati, effectively ensuring that he either learns the Gujarati text by heart or reinterprets it in his own form of speech
- asking questions and requesting answers in either or both languages
- asking for both translations and definitions
- discussing meaning
- making explicit reference to standard or literary forms of language with which Mohammed is not familiar
- retelling the story in his own words in both languages.

These strategies will be sufficient for parents who wish to read with their children and ensure their understanding, developing their oral language rather than literacy. To become an independent reader, however, Mohammed needs instruction in the Gujarati script and the nature of the writing system. At the point when the observation sessions ended, he was only just beginning this process.

Mydda was a good reader in English but, at the point where the observations started, she had made little progress with decoding the Urdu script. Bismah's strategies were focused around helping her to decode the text. These included:

- encouraging Mydda to read in English, telling her stories and rhymes and reading to her in Urdu
- initially using a very simple repetitive text to develop basic vocabulary and to draw attention to initial sounds in words and establish the learning of key letters in initial position
- ensuring Mydda had opportunities to speak Urdu with her extended family during the summer break
- providing a traditional Urdu primer with words, phrases and funny rhymes to illustrate sounds

- supporting decoding word by word and suggesting blending as Mydda does in English
- explaining word structures: the different forms of letters and the use of diacritics
- asking questions about meaning, discussing the text, encouraging Mydda to work out the Urdu before checking meaning with the English
- providing key vocabulary to fill in gaps in Mydda's knowledge and relating this to her experience and to cultural issues
- encouraging use of illustrations, environmental print
- locating a book of children's poems, modelling reading with expression and making good use of patterned language.

Mydda developed strong bottom-up strategies but her more limited knowledge of Urdu made prediction in reading difficult. Bismah noted that she needed to find time to read to her more regularly.

Both Mydda and Mohammed may have benefited from the use of transliteration as a stepping stone to learning to read the Urdu and Gujarati scripts.

Two of the case studies focused on children who were learning to read using dual language books without the benefit of adult support. The work of Lek and Durkan in Turkish and English demonstrates how, even if children have fairly limited reading skills in both languages, they can greatly benefit from working together and sharing their skills to decode and work out the meaning of the text. Both children had acquired an understanding of graphophonic principles in Turkish from an earlier brief attendance at complementary classes. They worked out their own strategies. These included:

- taking turns at reading in both languages and correcting each other
- reading together and discussing the meaning of words and sentences and relating these to personal cultural experiences
- focusing on the structure of words and sentences and discussing how Turkish and English differ
- working out meanings using graphophonic knowledge, guessing from the overall meaning of a sentence, using illustrations, using their knowledge of traditional stories to predict
- making up their own version of the story.

Lek was more dominant in English and Durkan in Turkish, but they were broadly matched in their abilities and their skills complemented each other.

The great benefit of this approach is that it enables children to hypothesise about language and reveals what they understand about the relationship between their languages. It is a very good activity to carry out in a classroom as part of language awareness work in which both bilingual and monolingual children explore dual language resources and make hypotheses about how language works.

Sarah, the solitary learner, also made up her own strategies and was virtually self- taught. She had the benefit of being a fluent speaker of two languages that have a shared script and many connections at the level of vocabulary. She was very highly motivated. Sarah was a very competent independent reader in both languages and was very good at working out the meaning of unfamiliar words from the context in both languages. She enjoyed interacting with the researcher, discussing the deeper meaning of texts, exploring the finer points of translation and making up extended versions of familiar stories. She would have greatly benefited from working with a partner and from regular access to advanced reading material in French. Sarah had had little opportunity to learn to write in French. As a keen and talented writer in English, bilingual book making would have developed her literacy skills.

Appendix
Practical ideas for the classroom: further reading

Redbridge Ethnic Minority Advisory Team: Developing Reading Skills through Home Languages

The research carried out by the teachers who participated in this study is described in this volume which is available from the children's services. It provides advice on how schools can create a reading culture that includes the use of home languages. The volume is accompanied by two CDs with printable resources for teachers wishing to establish a similar scheme. This includes:

- all resources used in the project including book reviews
- translated information
- reading skills addressed by the project
- advice on developing a whole school action plan

Jean Conteh: *Succeeding in Diversity*

Conteh notes that

'dual language texts have been available for children in schools in Britain for a long time, but their potential as teaching resources for all children may never have been fully realised.' (2003:151)

She suggests that children explore the parallel texts, their layout and features; make use of transliterations where available; discuss them bilingually; use them as a stimulus for writing stories that they know from their own cultures, and composing bilingual poems.

Charmian Kenner: *Becoming Biliterate*

Chapter 5 of this book, which describes 'literacy teaching systems in bilingual families', provides examples of the strategies that young bilingual children work out to teach their language to their classmates: modelling, guiding the hand for writing unfamiliar script, bilingual notices. It also recommends that, as well as encouraging children to produce bilingual writing in the classrooms, teachers encourage family members to support the children's bilingualism and children to teach their younger siblings, as well as providing information to families about resources available in the community.

Manjula Datta and Cathy Pomphrey: *A World of Languages: developing children's love of languages*

This book offers a mine of information on how to encourage children to explore languages in the classroom and how to make the best use of available bilingual adults. Classroom strategies include bilingual story telling, cross language work at the level of words, phrases and sentences, use of transliteration, ideas for mathematical activities. It suggests children use dual language books with different scripts to explore their features.

Charmian Kenner, Eve Gregory, Mahera Ruby and Salman Al-Azami: *Bilingual Learning for Second and Third Generation Children*

The authors stress the importance of providing bilingual learning in the mainstream classroom and offer the following guidance to teachers for developing the language skills of second and third generation bilingual children:

- use of transliteration as a bridge towards learning Bengali script
- presenting key vocabulary and language structures bilingually on the interactive whiteboard
- providing bilingual resources such as stories and poems in parallel versions, bilingual work cards and audio resources
- building partnerships with families to provide the children with support for the activities at home
- engaging the whole class in language awareness activities (2008b:131 -133).

Rosanna Raimato: *A Chance to Shine: The Languages Ladder – Using a Recognition Scheme with Heritage Languages other than English* (2005)

This paper describes a school-based project that used the Languages Ladder to recognise and record primary school children's skills in community languages through engaging with parents and the community. Published by CfBT at http://www.cfbt. com/evidenceforeducation/pdf/91091_ChanceToShine. pdf

Website resources

Using and Researching Dual Language Books for Children, a resource for teachers. University of East London, 2007

http://www.uel.ac.uk/education/research/duallanguagebooks/

The site was developed from a small action research project carried out by MA students and interested teachers in the Cass School of Education (2002-2004). It aims to promote the use of dual language books and other language materials in the classroom with a view to creating a bank of shared ideas and resources for teachers; to encourage undergraduates, student and trainee teachers and post graduate and research students who have an interest in bilingualism and multilingual issues to explore the potential of such materials as part of their research projects and to make their findings available to others; to work with publishers to evaluate multilingual materials and to stimulate the publication of new resources to meet the needs of pupils, parents and teachers.

Cummins *et al*, ELL Students Speak for Themselves: Identity Texts and Literacy Engagement in Multicultural Classrooms, 2006

http://www.curriculum.org/ secretariat/files/ELL identityTexts.pdf

The use of writing in two languages in the classroom has been developed as a means of exploring the fluctuating nature of personal identity in multilingual contexts. Practice and research in Canada have shown this process to be particularly supportive of children who have recently arrived in a new country and are coming to terms with a new language and a new culture.

Some very good examples of this work are available on the Dual Language Showcase site of Thornwood and Peel Schools. http://thornwood.peel schools.org/Dual/

Language of the month

http://www.newburypark.redbridge.sch. uk/langofmonth/

Winner of the European Award for Languages in 2005 and very highly recommended by anyone who has seen the programme in action! Joe Debono, an EMAG teacher at Newbury Park School, developed an exciting and innovative awareness of languages programme that has inspired many teachers in multilingual schools. Recordings, quizzes, booklets of classroom activities in 46 languages can all be downloaded free from http://www.newburypark. redbridge.sch.uk/langofmonth/index.html

March is Multilingual Month

Since it was launched in 1998, the concept of celebrating multilingualism in schools throughout the month of March has taken hold in many schools in London and beyond. The booklet *March is Multilingual Month* is full of information about languages, and ideas for introducing them to children in a very enjoyable way (Fahro Malik, 2009). www.multiverse.ac.uk/ViewArticle2. aspx?ContentId=13237

Hounslow Talking Stories Project – Dual Language Stories

Three very popular traditional stories have been produced as talking books in dual language versions using Clicker 4 (from Crick Software). *The Man, the Boy and the Donkey, The Hare and the Tortoise* and *Fox and Crane* are written in simple language, with attractive illustrations and good quality sound. Each of the stories is available in Punjabi, Arabic, Bengali, Albanian, Urdu, Portuguese, Hindi, Somali, Gujarati and British Sign Language. Each page has an illustration and two boxes with text, the first in English, the second in one of the ten available languages. There are buttons to click to hear the sound in both languages on the page. The stories can also be printed http://www.hvec. org.uk/ .

Dual language poems – Poems in Praise of Diversity – Bilingual Poems for the Classroom

A set of 45 posters (A4 size) with poems in two languages. A website dedicated to the poems was launched by Andrew Motion, the Poet Laureate, at the Nehru Centre in London on 22nd April 2008. All poems are available to download free from www. poemsfor.org. Audio recordings will be available later on the site.

Multilingual and Multicultural Resources from Espresso Primary

The CD contains three stories including *The Six Blind Men and the Elephant* in Arabic, English, Bengali, Urdu and Somali. They have clear and attractive illustrations, high quality sound and can be printed. They are accompanied by a wide range of resources for related activities. A story teller is seen engaging a class of young children with Anansi and Common Sense. http://www. espresso.co.uk/services/primary/index. html#Scene_1

Sites for stories from different cultures in a range of languages or in dual-text and multilingual activities and games:

- CILT, the National Centre for Languages, has grouped all information and teaching resources for primary languages on one site: http:// www.primary languages.org.uk/primary_languages.aspx

- http://www.bbc.co.uk/cbeebies/drilldown/stories/2/6/1/ – Around the World at CBeebies: Stories in languages from countries around the world. Available online in Arabic, Bengali, Cantonese, Danish, Gaelic, Hindi, Jamaican, Portuguese, Russian, Somali, Turkish, Welsh and Yoruba.
- www.blss.portsmouth.sch.uk – the website of Portsmouth Ethnic Minority Achievement Service has a leaflet on types on bilingualism. Under A-Z it has a treasure trove of resources in a wide range of languages: dual text stories (with sound), alphabet posters and numbers lines (with sound), number games and jig-saws etc

  www.bgfl.org/bgfl/ – on the Birmingham Grid for Learning site. A range of activities in Arabic, Bengali, Chinese, English, Somali and Urdu (body parts, fruit, tour of a virtual house, etc)
- www.bluemountainmedia.com – this is the site of a publisher of Caribbean folk tales (such as Anancy stories), proverbs and talking books for children. There are free examples on the website
- www.motherlandnigeria.com – this is an excellent site for language and cultural resources and children's literature. Go to kidzone. You will find about 50 full text traditional Nigerian (and other African) stories, games, dozens of proverbs, a wonderful collection of pictures and language resources in Yoruba, Ibo and Hausa
- http://a4esl.org/ – a site with multilingual quizzes for learners of English as an additional language. The bilingual vocabulary quizzes are fun and a welcome resource for language awareness activities. They are available in 36 languages
- http://www.bromley.org/ciswebpl/diversity/default.asp – a truly impressive resources site: 'This is the first LEA website of its kind in the UK, which not only catalogues hundreds of items available for loan, but also links each item with one or more relevant websites with teaching resources or interactive sites for students'

Publishers and suppliers of dual language books and multilingual resources for children

- www.mantralingua.com – the site of the leading publisher of dual language books for children. Mantra publishes books in 50 languages as well as interactive CD-ROMs, audio-CDs, posters, friezes and some toys, games and secondary curriculum-related teaching resources. Books include non-fiction and dictionaries. Publishers of the Talking Pen and the Recorder Pen. Mantra Lingua, Global House, Ballards Lane, London N12 8NP 020 8445 5123
- Milet Publishing www.milet.com publish children's dual language books in twenty languages. These include board books for young children, dictionaries and some audio-books. They are based in Chicago, but their books can be

ordered from: Turnaround Publisher Services, Unit 3, Olympia Trading Estate, Coburg Road, London N22 6TZ 020 8829 3000

- Learning Design Ltd, 020 7093 4051 www.learningdesign.biz
- RDS Books 020 8521 6969 www.rdsbooks.com
- Refugee Council Publications Unit, 240-250 Ferndale Road, London SW9 8BB – 020 7346 6738 or 020 7346 6732 www.refugeecouncil.org. uk/practice/eshop/folktales.htm (Regrettably these publications may now be difficult to obtain as the Refugee Council's education project had to cease due to lack of funding.)
- L'Harmattan, 5-7 Rue de l'école polytechnique, 75 005 Paris. Sales: 00 33 1 40 46 79 20 www.editions-harmattan.fr Publishers of dual language picture books for children in French and a wide range of African and far Eastern languages
- www.thai-bookshop.com Thai Books.This is not a dual language book site, but it does have a wonderful selection of books for children aged 0 to 9, and, as they say, 'other great stuff'
- www.chadpur-press.com dual language book and CD in Gujerati and English
- www.earlystart.co.uk publishes dual language books in French, Spanish and German with English and Big Book CD ROMs for use with whiteboards
- www.eastwestdiscovery.com is a US publisher and distributor of dual language texts for children with an extensive catalogue
- www.bramhallbooks.co.uk a small new family run publishing house. Books for young children in French and English with lesson plans freely downloadable from the website
- ww.yorubabooks.com a new publisher of children's books designed to teach Yoruba as a second language
- www.badger-publishing.co.uk have translated into Polish a selection of their popular titles for children aged 9 to 14. These are available in dual language format
- www.franceslincoln.com publishes an Urdu/English version of Mary Hoffman's Amazing Grace
- www.jubileebooks.co.uk a major supplier to schools has an extensive range of dual language books from different publishers. Showroom in Eltham, South London
- www.letterboxlibrary.com has a selection of dual language books for young children in a range of languages, most of them published by Mantralingua
- www.positive-identity.com/htm/books/dual_language_bks/duallangbks. htm Also supplies a range of dual language books published by Mantralingua.
- www.grantandcutler.com have a bookshop in central London. They have a good selection of children's fiction in European languages, including some in dual language format, and some children's books in other world languages

References

Ahlberg, J (1981) *Each Peach Pear Plum*. Hardmondsworth: Puffin

Ahlberg, J and A (1986) *The Jolly Postman or Other People's Letters*. London: Little Brown

Alcott, LM (1994) *Little Women*. London: Penguin Classics

Alcott, LM (1951) *Les Quatre Filles du Docteur March*. Paris: Hachette

Arshad, M (1999) *Pahlaa Qadam. Urdu Qaida*. Lahore: Khalid Publisher Urdu Bazar

Asan, H (2007) *Ceren's Love of Books*. London: Heyamola

Ashraf, K (2007) *The Fisherman and the Cat*. London: Chadpur Press

Ashraf, K (2008) *Why I started my bilingual publishing company, Chadpur Press*. http://www.uel.ac.uk/education/research/duallanguagebooks/what.htm. (accessed November 2008)

Bahl, U (1989) *Many Tales, Many Tongues: a bibliography of dual language books*. Waltham Forest: Multicultural Development Service

Baker, C (2006) *Foundations of Bilingual Education and Bilingualism*, 4th Edition. Clevedon: Multilingual Matters

Baker, P and Eversley, J (eds) (2000) *Multilingual Capital*. London: Battlebridge Publications

Bajraktari, I (2003) *Les neuf frères et le diable*. Paris: L'Harmattan

Barkow, H (2001a) *The Giant Turnip*. London: Mantra Lingua

Barkow, H (2001b) *The Three Billy Goats Gruff*. London: Mantra Lingua

Barkow, H (2002) *Beowulf*. London: Mantra Lingua

Barkow, H (2002) *The Pied Piper*. London: Mantra Lingua

Barton, D (1991) The social nature of writing. In Barton, D and Ivanic, R (eds) *Writing in the Community*. London: Sage

Barton, D (1994) *Literacy: An Introduction to the Ecology of Written Language*. Oxford: Blackwell

Bialystok, E (1997) Effects of bilingualism and biliteracy on children's emerging concepts of print. *Developmental Psychology* 33 (3) 429-440

Bialystok, E (2001) The extension of languages through other means. In Cooper, L, Shohamy, E and Walters, J *New Perspectives and Issues in Educational Language Policy*. Amsterdam/Philadelphia: John Benjamins.

Bialystok, E (2004) The impact of bilingualism on language and literacy development. In Bhatia, TK and Ritchie, WC (eds) *The Handbook of Bilingualism*. Oxford: Blackwell

Blackledge, A (2000) *Literacy, Power and Social Justice*. Stoke-on-Trent: Trentham Books

Blackledge, A (2004) Constructions of identity in political discourse in multilingual Britain. In Pavlenko, A and Blackledge, A (eds) *Negotiation of Identities in Multilingual Contexts*. Clevedon: Multilingual Matters.

Brooks, G, Gorman, T, Harman, J, Hutchinson, D and Wilkin, A (1996) *Family Literacy Works: the NFER Evaluation of the Basic Skills Agency's Demonstration Programmes.* London: Basic Skills Agency

Brown, J (2007) Getting started with primary languages: advice, support and resources for a multilingual approach. *Race Equality Teaching* 26 (1) 33-35

Browne, E (1994) *Handa's Surprise.* London: Mantra Lingua

Browne, E (2002) *Handa's Hen.* London: Mantra Lingua

Burningham, J (1984) *Mr Gumpy's Outing.* Hardmondsworth: Picture Puffin

Cable, C, Abji, H, Creese, A and Thompson, A (2009) *Developing a Bilingual Pedagogy for UK Schools.* Reading: NALDIC

Campbell, J (2008) Interview on 26th February 2008

Carle, E (1992) *The Very Hungry Caterpillar.* English and Gujarati. London: Mantra Lingua

Carter, R (2007) *The Man, the Boy and the Donkey.* http://www.hvec.org.uk/hvecmain/Sections/HLS/Docs/HLSstories/ManBoyDonk/MBDAlb/MBDTitle.htm (accessed October 2008)

Carter, R and Ahmed, R (2007) *The Six Blind Men and the Elephant.* London: Espresso Primary http://www.espresso.co.uk/services/primary/index.html#Scene_ (accessed October 2008)

Casey, D (2006) *Fox Fables.* London: Mantra Lingua

Casey, D (2006) *Isis and Osiris.* London: Mantra Lingua

Cbeebies, 2008. *Stories and Rhymes around the World.* BBC. http://www.bbc.co.uk/cbeebies/drilldown/stories/2/6/1/ (accessed October 2008)

Chana, U and Romaine, S (1984) Evaluative reactions to Panjabi/English code-switching. *Journal of Multilingual and Multicultural Development.* 5 (6) p447-473

CILT (2007) *Positively Plurilingual.* London: CILT, The National Centre for Languages

CILT, (2008) *Our Languages.* http://www.cilt.org.uk/commlangs/our_langs/ (accessed September 2008)

Clark, R, Fairclough, N, Ivanic, R and Martin-Jones, M (1990) Critical language awareness Part I: A critical review of three current approaches to language awareness. *Language and Education* 4 (4) 249-260

Clover, J and Gilbert, S (1981) Parental involvement in the development of language. *Multiethnic Education Review,* 3: 6-9

Clynes, K and Daykin, L (2003) *Not Again Red Riding Hood.* London: Mantra Lingua

Colledge, M and Campbell, J (1997) Grass roots views of dual language books. *IEDPE UK Newsletter* 4 5-7

Conteh, J (2003) *Succeeding in Diversity.* Stoke-on-Trent: Trentham Books.

Conteh, J (2007) Culture, language and learning: mediating a bilingual approach in complementary Saturday classes. In Conteh, J, Martin, P and Robertson, LH (eds) *Multilingual Learning Stories from Schools and Communities in Britain.* Stoke-on-Trent: Trentham Books

Conteh, J (2008) Miss, can you speak French? Linking 'MFL', 'EAL' and 'English' in primary language teaching. *Race Equality Teaching* 27 (1) 17-20

Conteh, J (2008) Interview on 21 February 2008

Conteh, J (forthcoming). Making links across complementary and mainstream classrooms for primary children and their teachers. In Lytra, V and Martin, P (eds) *Sites of Multilingualism: Complementary Schools in Britain today.* Stoke-on-Trent: Trentham Books

Conteh, J, Martin, P and Robertson, LH (2007) Multilingual learning stories from schools and communities in Britain: issues and debates. In Conteh, J, Martin, P and Robertson, LH (eds)

Multilingual Learning Stories from Schools and Communities in Britain. Stoke-on-Trent: Trentham Books

Creese, A, Bhatt, A, Bhojani, N and Martin, P (2006). Multicultural, heritage and learner identities in complementary schools. *Language and Education.* 20 (1) 23-43

Creese, A, Barac, T, Bhatt, A, Blackledge, A, Hamid, S, Lytra, V, Martin, P, Li Wei, Chao-Jung Wu, Yagcioglu-Ali, D (2008) *Investigating Multilingualism in Complementary Schools in Four Communities.* Birmingham: University of Birmingham

Cummins, J. (1984) *Bilingualism and Special Education: Issues in Assessment and Pedagogy.* Clevedon: Multilingual Matters.

Cummins, J (1986) Empowering minority students: a framework for intervention. *Harvard Educational Review.* 56 (1) 18-36

Cummins, J. (1991) Interdependence of first and second language proficiency in bilingual children. In Bialystok, E (ed) *Language Processing in Bilingual Children.* Cambridge: Cambridge University Press

Cummins, J (1996) *Negotiating Identities: Education for Empowerment in a Diverse Society.* Ontario, CA: California Association for Bilingual Education

Cummins, J (2000) *Language, Power and Pedagogy: Bilingual Children in the Crossfire.* Clevedon: Multilingual Matters

Cummins, J (2007) Evidence-based literacy strategies: bilingualism as a resource within the classroom. *Bilingualism, Learning and Achievement.* Conference at London Metropolitan University 3rd March 2007

Cummins, J, Swain, MK, Nakjima, K, Handscombe, J, Green, D, and Tran, C (1984). Linguistic interdependence among Japanese and Vietnamese in immigrant students. In Rivera, C, (ed) *Communicative Competence Approaches to Language Proficiency Assessment: Research and Application.* Clevedon: Multilingual Matters

Cummins, J, Bismilla, V, Chow, P, Cohen, S, Giampapa, F, Leoni, L, Sandhu, P, and Sastri, P (2006) *ELL Students Speak for Themselves: Identity Texts and Literacy Engagement in Multilingual Classrooms* http://www.curriculum.org/secretariat/files/ELLidentityTexts.pdf (accessed June 2008)

Datta, M (ed) (2007) *Bilinguality and Literacy.* (2nd edn) London: Continuum

Datta, M and Pomphrey, C (2004) *A World of Languages: Developing Children's Love of Languages.* London: CILT

Debono, J (2002) *Language of the Month.* http://www.newburypark.redbridge.sch.uk/langofmonth/ (accessed December 2008)

Department for Children, Schools and Families, 2007. *Guidance on the Duty to Promote Community Cohesion.* London: DCSF

Department of Education and Science (1985) *Education for All (The Swann Report).* London: HMSO

Department for Education and Employment (2000) *The National Curriculum KS1 and KS2 Handbook for Primary Teachers in England.* London: DfEE/QCA

Department for Education and Skills (2003) *Aiming High: Raising the Achievement of Minority Ethnic Pupils.* Annesley, Notts: DfES

Department for Education and Skills (2002) *Languages for All, Languages for Life.* Annesley, Notts: DfES

Department for Education and Skills (2005) *Every Child Matters.* Annesley, Notts: DfES

Department for Education and Skills (2005) *The Key Stage 2 Framework for Languages* http://nationalstrategies.standards.dcsf.gov.uk/primary/publications/languages/framework/ (accessed January 2009)

Department for Education and Skills (2006) *Learning and Teaching for Bilingual Children in the Primary Years.* Annesley, Notts: DfES

Desai, N (1989) *The Raja's Big Ears.* London: Jennie Ingham Associates

Edwards, V (1998) *The Power of Babel: Teaching and Learning in Multilingual Classrooms.* Stoke-on-Trent: Trentham Books

Edwards, V (2009) *Learning to be Literate, Multilingual Perspectives.* Clevedon: Multilingual Matters

Edwards,V and Walker, S (1996) Some status issues in the translation of children's books. *Journal of Multilingual and Multicultural Development* 17(5) 339-348

Edwards, V, Pemberton, L, Knight, J and Monaghan, F (2002) Fabula: A bilingual multimedia authoring environment for children exploring minority languages. *Language Learning and Technology* 6(2) 59-69

Ernst-Slavit, G and Mulhern, M (2006) *Bilingual Books: Promoting Literacy and Biliteracy in the Second-Language and Mainstream Classroom.* http://www.readingonline.org/articles/ernst-slavit/index.html (accessed October 2008)

Ethnic Minority Achievement Team (2008) *Developing Reading Skills through Home Language Project.* London Borough of Redbridge: EMAT

Faltis, CJ (1995) Building bridges between parents and the school. In Garcia, O and Baker, C (eds) *Policy and Practice in Bilingual Education.* Clevedon: Multilingual Matters

Fernandez Lopez, M (2000) Translation studies in contemporary children's literature: A comparison of intercultural and ideological factors. In G Lathey (ed) *The Translation of Children's Literature.* Clevedon: Multilingual Matters

Fishman, JA (1980) Language maintenance and ethnicity. In Fishman, JA (1989) *Language and Ethnicity in Minority Sociolinguistic Perspective.* Clevedon: Multilingual Matters

Gijubhai (1973) *Soopad kanna Rajani varta.* Bombay and Ahmedabad: Seth

Gonzales, N, Moll, Z, Floyd-Tenery, M, Rivera, A, Rendon, P, Gonzales, R, Andante, C (1993) *Teacher Research on Funds of Knowledge: Learning from Households.* www.ncela.qwu.edu/pubs/cvrcdsll//epr6.htm (accessed May 2007)

Goodman, K (1996) *On Reading: A Common-sense Look at the Nature of Language and the Science of Reading.* Portsmouth, NH: Heinemann

Grange Road First School (1993) *Send for Sohail.* Bradford: Partnership Publishing, Bradford and Ilkley Community College

Gravelle, M (1996) *Supporting Bilingual Learners in Schools.* Stoke-on-Trent: Trentham Books

Gravelle,M. (2000) Mufaro's beautiful daughters: promoting first languages within the context of the literacy hour. In Gravelle, M (ed) *Planning for Bilingual Learners – an inclusive curriculum.* Stoke-on-Trent: Trentham Books

Gregory, E (2008a) Interview on 25th March 2008

Gregory, E (2008b) *Learning to Read in a New Language.* London: Sage

Gregory, E and Biarnès, J (1994) Tony and Jean François: looking for sense in the strangeness of school, in Dombey, H and Meek-Spencer, M (eds) *First Steps Together: Home-School Early Literacy in European Contexts.* Stoke-on-Trent: Trentham/IEDPE

Gregory, E, Long, S and Volk, D (2004). Syncretic literacy studies: starting points. In Gregory, E, Long, S and Volk, D (eds) *Many Pathways to Literacy.* London: RoutledgeFalmer

Gregory, E and Penman, D (1985) *The Fisherman and his Wife and other Wishing Tales.* London: Edward Arnold

Gregory, E, Lathwell, J, Mace, J, and Rashid, N (1993) *Literacy at Home and at School. Report of a Research Study (1992-1993).* London: Goldsmiths College, Unversity of London.

REFERENCES

Gregory, E and Williams, A (2000) *City Literacies. Learning to Read across Generations and Cultures.* London: Routledge

Gregory, M (2004) *Jill and the Beanstalk.* London: Mantralingua

Hall, S (1992) New ethnicities. In Rattansi, A and Donald, J. *Culture and Difference.* London: Sage

Hamers, JF and Blanc, MHA (1989) *Bilinguality and Bilingualism.* Cambridge: Cambridge University Press

Hancock, R (1993) Introduction. In Korel, E *Kurdish Folktales.* London: Hackney PACT

Hancock, R (1995) Hackney PACT, Home reading programmes and family literacy. In Raban-Bisby, B, Brooks, G and Wolfendale, S (eds) *Developing Language and Literacy.* Stoke-on-Trent: Trentham/UKRA

Hancock, R (2007) Interview 17th December 2007

Harris, R (1997) Romantic bilingualism: time for a change? In Leung, C and Cable, C (eds) *English as an Additional Language, Changing Perspectives.* Watford: NALDIC

Harris, R (2006) *New Ethnicities and Language Use.* Basingstoke: Palgrave Macmillan

Hergé (2005) *Tintin in the Congo.* Glasgow: Egmont

Hill, E (1984) *Where's Spot? English and Bengali version.* London: Roy Yates Books

Holdaway, D (1979) *The Foundations of Literacy.* New-York: Ashton-Scholastic

Hornberger, N (2000) Multilingual literacies, literacy practices, and the continua of biliteracy. In Martin-Jones, M and Jones, K (eds) *Multilingual Literacies.* Amsterdam: John Benjamins

Ingham, J (1986) *Telling Tales Together.* London: The Cadmean Trust

Jabeen, Z (1992) *The Moving Mango Tree.* Bradford: Partnership Publishing, Bradford and Ilkley Community College.

John, C (2007) *Writing and illustrating a personal version of a favourite family story from the home country* http://www.uel.ac.uk/education/research/duallanguagebooks/why.htm (accessed October 2008)

Jones, M (1996) *The Balloon Detectives.* Bradford: Partnership Publishing, Bradford and Ilkley Community College

Kabra, K (2007) *Developing communication: parents, children and trainee teachers working on dual language materials.* Multiverse: http://www.multiverse.ac.uk/attachments/a91eb6c1-a529-46c9-a2b9-ae8dbb02e37b.ppt (accessed September 2008)

Kenner, C (2000a) *Home Pages. Literacy Links for Bilingual Children.* Stoke-on-Trent: Trentham Books

Kenner, C (2000b) Children writing in a multilingual nursery. In Martin-Jones, M and Jones, K (eds) *Multilingual Literacies.* Amsterdam: John Benjamins

Kenner, C (2004) *Becoming Biliterate: Young Children Learning Different Writing Systems.* Stoke-on-Trent: Trentham Books

Kenner, C, Arju, T, Gregory, E, Jessel, J, Ruby, M, (2004) The Role of grandparents in children's learning. *Primary Practice,* 38 (Autumn) 41-45

Kenner, C, Creese, A and Francis, B (2008a) Language, identity and learning in complementary schools. *CILT Community Languages Bulletin* 22, Spring 2008 2-4

Kenner, C, Gregory, E, Ruby, M, Al-Azami, S (2008b) Bilingual learning for second and third generation children. *Language, Culture and Curriculum* 21(2) 120-137

Kenner, C, Al-Azami, S, Gregory, E, Ruby, M (2008c) Bilingual poetry: expanding the cognitive and cultural dimensions of children's learning. *Literacy* 42(2) 92-100.

Knight, I (2007) Let Tintin the Racist speak. *Sunday Times,* July 15th http://www.timesonline.co.uk/tol/comment/columnists/india_knight/article2076264.ece (accessed March 2009)

Lathey, G (2006) *The Translation of Children's Literature*. Clevedon: Multilingual Matters

Li Wei (1994) *Three Generations, Two Languages, One Family. Language Choice and Language Shift in a Chinese Community in Britain*. Clevedon: Multilingual Matters

Linguistic Minorities Report (1985) *The Other Languages of England: The Linguistic Minorities Report*. London: Routledge and Kegan Paul

Ma, J (2008) Learning to read as a collaborative enterprise. *Education 3-13* 36(3)

Malik, F (2009) *March is Multilingual Month.* (10th edn). London: Lynkreach www.multiverse.ac.uk/ViewArticle2.aspx?ContentId=13237

Martin, B (2004) *Brown Bear, Brown Bear, What Do You See?* London: Mantra Lingua

Martin, PW, Bhatt, A, Bhojani, N and Creese, A (2006) Managing bilingual interaction in a Gujarati complementary school in Leicester. *Language and Education* 20 (1) 5-22

Martin-Jones, M and Jones, K (2000). Multilingual literacies. In Martin-Jones, M and Jones, (eds) *Multilingual Literacies*. Amsterdam: John Benjamins

Meek, M (1988) *How Texts Teach what Readers Learn.* Stroud: Thimble Press

Meek, M (ed) (2001) *Preface. In Children's Literature and National identity.* Stoke-on-Trent: Trentham

Mehmedbegovic, D (2007) London's multilingual schools. In Brighouse, T and Fullick, L (eds) *Essays from London: Education in a Global City*. London: Institute of Education

Mills, D (2000) *Lima's Red Hot Chilli.* London: Mantra Lingua

Ming Tsow (1986) Dual language text or not. *Language Matters* (3) 13-17

Mullis, L (2007) *Promoting Children's Home Languages in an East London Nursery School* http://www.multiverse.ac.uk/ViewArticle2.aspx?Keyword=Mullis&SearchOption=And&SearchType=Keyword&RefineExpand=1&ContentId=13748 (accessed October 2008)

Multilingual Resources for Children Project (1995) *Building Bridges: Multilingual Resources for Children.* Clevedon: Multilingual Matters with the University of Reading

O'Connel, E (1999) Translating for children. In Lathey, G (ed) *The Translation of Children's Literature*. Clevedon: Multilingual Matters

O'Sullivan, E (2001) Alice in different wonderlands. In Meek, M (ed) *Children's Literature and National Identity*. Stoke-on-Trent: Trentham

Office for Standards in Education (2005) *Could they do even better? The Writing of Advanced Bilingual Learners of English at KS2 – HMI Survey of Good Practice.* (HMI 2452) London: OfSTED

Office for Standards in Education, (2008) *Every Language Matters. An evaluation of the extent and impact of initial training to teach a wider range of world languages.* London: OfSTED

Office for Standards in Education (2008) *Henry Maynard Infants' School Inspection Report* http://www.ofsted.gov.uk/oxedu_reports/display/(id)/103666 (Accessed September 2008)

PACT (Parents and Children and Teachers), (1984) *Home-School Reading Partnerships in Hackney.* London: Inner London Education Authority

Patel, (1974) *Rupa the Elephant.* New Delhi: National Book Trust

Pavlenko, A and Blackledge, A (2004). New theoretical approaches to the study of negotiation of identities in multilingual contexts. In Pavlenko, A and Blackledge, A (eds) *Negotiation of Identities in Multilingual Contexts*. Clevedon: Multilingual Matters

Pim, C (2008) Multi-modal literacies: developing the 'Talking Pen' to meet the distinctive needs of students learning English as an additional language. *NALDIC Quarterly* 5(3) 13-15

Puurtinen, T (1994) Translating children's literature: theoretical approaches and empirical studies. In Lathey, G (ed) (2006) *The Translation of Children's Literature*. Clevedon: Multilingual Matters

REFERENCES

Raimato, R (2005) *A Chance to Shine: The Languages Ladder – Using a Recognition Scheme with Heritage Languages other than English.* CfBT http://www.cfbt.com/evidenceforeducation/pdf/ 91091_ ChanceToShine.pdf (accessed November 2007)

Rashid, N and Gregory, E (1997) Learning to read, reading to learn: the importance of siblings in the language development of young bilingual children. In Gregory, E (ed) *One Child, Many Worlds: Early Learning in Multicultural Communities.* London: David Fulton

Robert, N (2002) *The Swirling Hijab.* London: Mantra Lingua

Robert, N (2005) *A Journey through Islamic Arts.* London: Mantra Lingua

Robertson, LH (2006) Learning to Read 'properly' by moving between parallel literacy classes. *Language and Education* 20 (1) 44-61

Rowling, JK (1997) *Harry Potter and the Philosopher's Stone* London: Bloomsbury

Rowling, JK (1998) *Harry Potter à l'école des sorcières.* Paris: Folio Junior

Shankar, 1981 *The Woman and the Crow.* New Delhi: Children's Book Trust

Shavit, Z (1986) Translation of children's literature. In Lathey, G (ed) *The Translation of Children's Literature.* Clevedon:Multilingual Matters

Solbakk, JT (1994) *Maya Sami.* Karasjok: Davvi Girji os

Sneddon, R (1986a) The mother and child writing group. *Language Matters*, (2) 18-23

Sneddon, R (1986b) Allwrite in Hackney. *ILEC. Journal* Spring 1 14-15

Sneddon, R (1997) Working towards partnership: parents, teachers and community organisations. In Bastiani, J (ed) *Home-School Work in Multicultural Settings.* London: David Fulton

Sneddon, R (2000) Language and literacy practices in Gujarati Muslim families. In Martin-Jones, M and Jones, K (eds) *Multilingual Literacies.* Amsterdam: John Benjamins

Sneddon, R and Patel, K (2003) The Raja's big ears, the journey of a story across cultures. *Language and Education* 17(5) 371-384

Sneddon, R (2007) *Using and researching dual language books* http://www.uel.ac.uk/education/ research/duallanguagebooks/arp.htm (accessed January 2009)

Stone, S (1989) *The Naughty Mouse.* London: Jennie Ingham Associates

Street, B (1984). *Literacy in Theory and Practice.* Cambridge: Cambridge University Press.

Street, B (2000). Literacy events and literacy practices: theory and practice in the New Literacy Studies. In Martin-Jones, M and Jones, K (eds) *Multilingual Literacies.* Amsterdam: John Benjamins

Street, B (1993) *Cross-cultural Approaches to Literacy.* Cambridge: Cambridge University Press

Synek, J and M (2008) *Où es-tu Petit Loup?* Seaton: Bramhall Publishing

Thomas, W and Collier, V (2002) *A National Study of School Effectiveness for Language Minority Students' Long-term Academic Achievement.* Centre for Research on Education, Diversity and Excellence (CREDE) http://www.crede.ucs.edu.research/llaa/1.1_final.html

Tizard, J, Schofield WN and Hewison, J (1982) Collaboration between teachers and parents in assisting children's reading. *British Psychological Society* 52 (1) 1-5

Townsend, HER (1971) *Immigrant Pupils in England, the LEA Response.* Slough: NFER

Troyna, B. and Williams, J. (1986) *Racism, Education and the State: the racialisation of education policy.* London: Routledge

Tubassam, SGM (1998) *Ab sub hein toat batoat mian.* Lahore: Alfaisal Urdu Bazar

Vega, D (1997) Jill and the Beanstalk. In Lansky, B (ed) *Newfangled Fairy Tales.* New-York: Meadowbank Press

Walker, B (1984) *Naughty Imran.* Urdu translation by Khan, T; Waltham Forest: Multicultural Development Service

Walker, B (1996) Jill and the Beanroot. In *Feminist Fairy Tales*. San Francisco: Harper

Welch, A (2009) Interview on 6th March 2009

Welch, J (2009) Interview on 6th March 2009

Williams, A (1997) Investigating literacy in London: three generations of readers in an East End family. In Gregory, E (ed) *One Child, Many Worlds: Early Learning in Multicultural Communities*. London: David Fulton

Wyse, D and Goswami, U (2009) Synthetic phonics and the teaching of reading. *British Educational Research Journal* 34 (6) 691-710

Index

action research 19, 21, 142
Ashraf, Keya 17, 25

Beowulf 115
Bialystok, Ellen 33-34
bilingualism
    additive – subtractive 30
    benefits and challenges
    32
    definition 28-29
bilingual education/bilingual
    learning 37-38, 142
biliteracy 36-37, 143-144
    see also multiliteracy
book making 3, 47-49, 80-81,
    144
Bradford Partnership
    Publishing 11, 48-49, 80-
    81
*Brown Bear, Brown Bear,
    what do you see?* 87

Campbell, Janet 6-7
Clover, Jaqui 1-3
Common Underlying
    Proficiency 33
community Languages 35, 37
complementary Schools/
    mother tongue schools
    35, 37, 46
Conteh, Jean 12
Cummins, Jim 43

developing reading skills
    through home languages
    21, 69, 143

dual language books
    evaluation 21-22
    identity 47-49
    issues in translation 60
    117-118
    purpose and function 57
    research 18, 20, 38-39
    see also action research
    sharing culture 65

empowerment 35, 82-83

family literacy 36-37, 41, 45,
    86, 127, 144
The Fisherman and the Cat
    17, 136
Framework for Languages 17
funds of knowledge 40

The Giant Turnip 100
Gilbert, Sue 1-3
Gravelle, Maggie 22
Gregory, Eve 7

Hancock, Roger 10-11, 58
Handa's Hen 73
Handa's Surprise 94-95
Harris, Roxy 45
*Harry Potter and the
    Philosopher's Stone* 116
Hornberger, Nancy 36

identity
    affirming 43, 47
    language 44-46, 50, 82, 95
    learner 46, 51-52, 97,
    110, 124, 139

multicultural 51, 53, 95
multidimensional 44, 50
    negotiating 43
    personal/cultural 43, 45,
    46-47, 58, 111
identity texts 35, 48
Ingham, Jennie 8-9

John, Claire 4

Kenner, Charmian 37, 142

language awareness 24, 144
language shift/loss 29-30, 71
language use (patterns of)
    31, 70-71, 85-86, 113,
    143-144
languages (relationship
    between) 33-34, 63, 72,
    88, 125, 136
Little Women 118

Ma, James 20, 47
making books *see* book
    making
Mantra 13
Meek, Margaret 99
metalinguistic skills 7, 104-
    105, 125
Ming Tsow 18
Mother and Child Writing
    Group 3
The Moving Mango Tree 93
multilingual curriculum 45, 47
Multilingual Resources for
    Children 19-20

multiliteracy/multiliteracies 36, 38 see biliteracy
multi-media 13/14

National Languages Strategy
The Naughty Mouse 129
Newham Women's Community Writing Group 7
Not Again, Red Riding Hood 77, 114

PACT (Parents and Children and Teachers) 10, 39
Pahlaa Qadam 89
parents/siblings/ grandparents (partnerships with) 5-6, 9, 39-40
The Pied Piper 119

The Raja's Big Ears 131
reading strategies 131-136, 145-148
    collaborative 100
    decoding 72-74, 87-88, 93, 100-101, 134
    making meaning 75-79, 117, 129-130
    negotiating meaning 77, 105
    retelling stories 119-122, 134
Reading Materials for Minority Groups Project 8
research *see* action research

Shavit, Zohar 59
Swann report 35
The Swirling Hijab 72
syncretic literacy 36

Talking Pen/ Recorder pen 16
transfer of skills 33-34
translation
    cultural issues 64
    issues in language structure 63
    language choices 58, 62
    models 59
    purpose and function 56
    school-based 4-6
see also dual language books – issues in translation

Welsh, Amanda 25
Welsh, John 8
writing
    invented spelling 123
    re-telling story 123
    writing workshops 4, 7